JERSEY SHORE POETS
FIRST EDITION

Jersey Shore Poets

FIRST EDITION

A writers group anthology (with additional contributions)

Edited by Christopher Bogart and Gregg G. Brown

Introduction by Christopher Bogart

To Jonathan, From the founder of Jersey Shore Poets to a future Jersey Shore Poet.

Chris Bogart

Published by BLAST PRESS
324B Matawan Avenue
Cliffwood, NJ 07721
(732) 970-8409

ISBN 978-0-99848-290-3

"And All the Peasants Cheered for the King. The End." from
Jackleg Opera: Collected Poems, 1990 to 2013 by BJ Ward,
published by North Atlantic Books, copyright © 2013 by BJ
Ward. Reprinted by permission of publisher.

Cover painting is by Ken Ahlering.

NOTE ON THE COVER ART

Ken Ahlering is an artist who has specialized in oil paintings for over sixty years. His works are highly representational and focus on both land and seascapes, primarily of the seasonal Vermont hills and the Jersey Shore, in all its remarkable moods. Frequently he ventures off to explore other unique themes just to refresh his inspiration. His simple goal is to make paintings that quiet a room and start a conversation.

This November scene of the beautiful dunes at New Jersey's Island Beach State Park selected for the cover of this book was also previously chosen by the U.S. State Department for its "Art at the Embassies" program. It was initially displayed at the U.S. Embassy in Uzbekistan and is currently prominently displayed at the U.S. Embassy in Kazakhstan.

Ken considers it an honor for the Jersey Shore Poets to have chosen this image as their banner.

More of Ken's work can be viewed at ken-ahlering.com

CONTENTS

Theresa Irwin

Charles H. Johnson

Victoria Kaloss

X. J. Kennedy

Adele Kenny

H. A. Maxson

Laura McCullough

D. J. Moores

Anna Moran

Patrick Moran

Mihaela Moscaliuc

Linda Johnston Muhlhausen

Peter E. Murphy

C. John Schoonejongen

Lauren Schmidt

Jennifer E. Stahl

Jersey Shore Poets is a poetry writing group, now in its seventh year, that meets once a month at the Eatontown Library.

The purpose of the group is to provide a supportive environment for local working poets in the Monmouth County area to write, revise and critique their writing, to provide information, feedback and support to hone their craft as well as to seek various opportunities for public reading and publishing. The group also encourages and promotes the writing and appreciation of poetry through various local readings and instructional events.

Each meeting, a different member facilitates the group, providing one timed prompt for free-writing, and a "homework" assignment for further practice. Poets bring copies of one poem they wish to share with the group, and receive criticism/feedback from the group to help improve the poem. All the writer needs for these meetings is 12 copies of an original poem, a writing implement and paper or a notebook. The meetings usually last from 7:00 PM to 9:00 PM.

Each April, in celebration of National Poetry Month, JSP hosts an event called "Poets Live!" at the Monmouth County Library/Eastern Branch that features two renowned and published poets. Each member of JSP also is given time to read at the event, and an open mic follows. This event too is in its sixth year.

This year, for the first time, JSP has published an anthology, *Jersey Shore Poets / First Edition*, which includes not only of the written work of its twelve members, but also the work of over thirty five renowned poets and writers, a group that includes two US Poet Laureates as well as three Pulitzer Prize winners.

Jersey Shore Poets always welcomes new members.

If you would like more information on the group or wish to attend the next meeting, please email Chris Bogart at jerseyshorepoets@gmail.com or look on Facebook under the name Jersey Shore Poets at facebook.com/#!/JerseyShorePoets.

INTRODUCTION

One dark, not stormy but very cold, night on January 4, 2011 to be precise, I gathered five working poets together at seven o'clock in the evening in the public meeting room at the Eatontown Public Library to discuss the formation of a new poetry group. On the top of the sparse agenda, I had typed: "The New Poetry Group," a temporary placeholder for a name for our new group. I had no preconceived notions of what I wanted this group to be — just that it would be a source of inspiration and creative thought for writers like me who understood how difficult it was sometimes to write alone — with no feedback, no encouragement. I guess what I was looking for was a support group of sorts, a place of both security and productivity. Well, that night, we had a productive first meeting, discussing the attributes our poetry group would need to have in order to help us grow as working poets and writers. At our next meeting, in February, we chose the name we would be known by for the next six years: Jersey Shore Poets.

As word spread that Monmouth County had a new poetry group, others joined us until the group settled into its present number of twelve. It had been thirteen but, sadly, one of those first members, Jay Bradwein, a soft-spoken slam poet, left us far too soon on October 9, 2015 at the age of thirty-nine.

Over the ensuing six years, JSP has continued to meet one night each month, even on dark *and* stormy ones, at the meeting room of the Eatontown Public Library to share our work and to offer support and encouragement to each other on our journey as writers. We have also gone beyond the confines of that room to host poetry readings at the Monmouth County

Library/Eastern Branch every April for National Poetry Month, when we invite two feature readers from among the larger poetic community to share their work with us and our audiences. Each Jersey Shore Poet is given time on that day to read their own work, and an open mic is offered to encourage our audiences to get involved. The event is called *Poets Live!* and has become increasingly more successful and more popular with each passing year.

This anthology, then, is another way we have chosen to move beyond that meeting room of the Eatontown Public Library and to share our efforts with the world. By the title of this anthology, *Jersey Shore Poets/First* Edition, you might think that this is a collection of writing about the Jersey shore, but it is oh so much more than that!

First, as the subtitle indicates, it is our first edition, our first effort to be heard. If you listen really carefully, you might hear yourself saying with Susan Martin in her poem, "Whale Song," that *At first all I heard was a cacophony of random music, but as I listened, I found myself humming ...* then, as you read on, you'll discover that the scope of the poems in this book go beyond the parameters of Anna Moran's memory in her poem, "An Irishman's Thoughts," *Hurts are its flagstone floor. The future, its windows. The roof, its limits.* Whether offering a majestic invitation, *Come dream beside me by the gentle fire, that roared old monarchs to the brink* ("The Poet to His Countrymen" by Gregg Glory), or relating the teen angst of a first love, *Would she come to the window, I would wonder and then glance once and then again, hoping for a miracle* ("My First Love" by Patrick Moran), or of first lust, *You slid through my soul like a snake on silk. Helpless, I grabbed you and hung on* ("Desire" by S.O. Schiro), you will find that the poems in this volume speak to the reader in a variety of unique ways.

From a spring shower, *When rain quenches dirt and the sweetness emerges* ("Sweet Memories" by Victoria Kaloss), to a summer reverie, *Willow branches hang heavy, their blue shadows an awning over the ancient clothesline* ("First Bloom" by Jennifer Stahl), an autumnal interruption, *brief gusts of wind on brittle branches, tapping tattoos against frozen window panes* ("A Poem is a Stone" by Christopher Bogart), to winter in all its wonders, *First snow ... Forgives the earth. Its cold reveals the warmth of linen hills* ("First Snowfall" by Jerome Leary), these poems look beyond the Jersey shores of summer to all seasons of the wide world beyond its Atlantic sands.

So I suggest that, before you begin to read this volume of poetry and prose, you leave your preconceived notions about a book of writing you might think would be about the Jersey Shore, and be prepared instead to be taken beyond *that limbo between night and day,* (where) *light nudges heavy and resisting dark,* ("Wakeup call" Linda Johnston Muhlhausen) and toward that place where *stealthily comes tomorrow's dawn in silent steady streams* ("A Faded Rose" Theresa Irwin).

Finally, as if all of this diversity were not enough, we have the honor to be joined in this volume by over thirty national and world-renowned poets and writers, including three Pulitzer Prize winners and two United States Poets Laureate, who have generously agreed to share some of their work with us to make our first effort a particularly unique one.

We offer, then, this very special anthology to you, dear reader, to share with you what drives us to put pen to paper (or fingers to keys) each and every day, to dare what the character in C. John Schoonejongen's poem "A Million Streaks of Light" dares:

I see myself through a prism, he said,
A million streaks of light,
Not whole, never whole.
I'm spoiling for a fight
With those who stole my story and threw it to a brutal wind;
My "I am" spread among the stars at night.

Christopher Bogart
Founder
Jersey Shore Poets
December 2016

James Arthur

ODE TO AN ENCYCLOPEDIA

O hefty hardcover on the built-in shelf in my parents' living room,
O authority stamped on linen paper, molted from your dustjacket,
Questing Beast of blue and gold, you were my companion

on beige afternoons that came slanting through the curtains
behind the rough upholstered chair. You knew how to trim a sail
and how the hornet builds a hive. You had a topographical map

of the mountain ranges on the far side of the moon
and could name the man who shot down the man
who murdered Jesse James. At forty, I tell myself

that boyhood was all enchantment: hanging around the railway,
getting plastered on cartoons; I see my best friend's father
marinating in a lawn chair, smiling benignly at his son and me

from above a gin and tonic, or perched astride his roof
with carpentry nails and hammer, going at some problem
that kept resisting all his mending. O my tome, my paper brother,

my narrative without an ending, you had a diagram
of a cow broken down into the major cuts of beef,
and an image of the Trevi Fountain. The boarding house,

the church on the corner: all that stuff is gone.
In winter in Toronto, people say, a man goes outside
and shovels snow mostly so that his neighbors know

just how much snow he is displacing. I'm writing this
in Baltimore. For such a long time, the boy wants to grow up
and be at large, but posture becomes bearing;

bearing becomes shape. A man can make a choice
between two countries, believing all the while
that he will never have to choose.

Renée Ashley

SALT TO MAKE A SEA

I cannot hold such emptiness
—the only meaning, the meaning

we make & the way time tugs
the body down, the body named

bone, named brain, the color
of dust and tremor, the soft meat

and the bag it lives in. We beg
from the body; it shivers and

spits—we settle for desire, in-
commensurate sorrow, for a life

like too much water, shallow & wide,
for enough salt to make a little sea.

Christopher Bogart

Christopher Bogart is a retired educator and a working poet and writer with an MA in Creative Writing from Monmouth University.

He is the founder and a member of *Jersey Shore Poets*, and organizes an annual public poetry reading for National Poetry Month, "Poets Live!" at Monmouth County Library/Eastern Branch.

His poetry has been published in *Voices Rising from the Grove, Spindrift, WestWard Quarterly, Saggio Poetry Journal, The Monmouth Review* (2013 and 2014), *Mind Murals* (2013), *Whirlwind Review* (Fall 2014), *The Howl of Sorrow, a Collection of Poetry Inspired by Hurricane Sandy, This Broken Shore* (Summer 2015) as well as on various online sites.

As a published writer, his music and concert reviews have appeared in *Back Stage Pass* (July 1984, August 1984), His review of the first book of poetry by Natalie Diaz, *When My Brother Was an Aztec*, was published in *Pleiades Journal* (Winter 2014). In 2015, he was chosen as First Runner Up for Monmouth University's inaugural *The Joyce Carol Oates Award for Excellence in Fiction, Poetry, and Creative Non-Fiction.*

On August 1, 2005, he presented a paper on the importance of poetry in the teaching of literature and writing to the Oxford Round Table at the Oxford Union Debate Hall at Oxford University.

He is presently writing poetry and short stories, translates poetry from Spanish and French, as well as working on his first novel, tentatively titled *The Beast*, about the plight of two Central American teenage migrants who flee poverty and crime in search of a better life.

IN THE GLOAMING

In the gloaming,
Black cut-out silhouettes
Stand stark
Against the fading cerulean sky.

In the gloaming,
Fireflies rise in the cool night air
To hover there,
Winking in the gathering darkness.

In the gloaming,
We stand with our feet against the final line.
Our eyes seek out the flight of dying light
To reach the fleeting edge of our eternity.

A POEM IS A STONE

A poem is a stone
Skimmed over still waters
Leaving concentric circles
In its near perfect wake.

A poem is a gentle breeze
That rustles dry leaves,
Releasing them from distant trees
And sending them on their journey
To the frozen ground below.

Poems are brief gusts of wind
On brittle branches, tapping tattoos
Against frozen window panes
In vain attempts to enter.

Poetry is symphony.
Its sonorous sounds
Resound
Like the lone bow stroke of a cello,
Excite
Like the flight of slender fingers
Plucking willingly on heart strings,
Borne
On the throaty notes of an English horn.

Poems pound the brain
Like mental rain,
Forming puddles in the mind that
Slowly saturate its soil,
There to boil in deep wells of thought
Bought by the sounds
That abound
Around words.

MAYPOPS

Passiflora incarnata

One March in southern fields near Alcolu,
George Stinney and his sister grazed their cow.
Two white girls passed in search of maypop flowers.
Their battered bodies late that day were found.

One hundred volunteers commenced a search.
Two black boys fit the chosen race profile.
Three policemen settled finally on just one—
A ninety-two pound fourteen year old child.

From each core, maypop flowers grow five limbs.
To scare the Stinney family took just four.
Three policemen lied with oaths to seal his fate.
Two massive voltage surges did the chore.

George shuddered twice; one clear tear stained each cheek.
Old Sparky's metal mask bounced off the floor.

PONY RIDE

Behold the Lamb of God, that taketh away the sin of the world.
                                        ~~John 1:29

The boy, almost eighteen, sits on the damp concrete of a
        narrow alleyway,
His legs tucked up in a fetal position,
The open toes of his worn black sneakers
Jammed against the cold brick wall,
His back pressed against an old wooden door.

He nudges the cleft of his chin against the collar of a dirty
    jeans jacket.
His thick fingers fumble eagerly for his kit
As he hums a tune softly,
A tune from a 50's TV show he's never seen.

His hollowed eyes,
Once the beautiful warm brown of a chestnut colt,
Are now pale and vacant,
Able to see nothing but the rubber tubing, the black plastic
    lighter,
The tarnished spoon
And the white plastic syringe,
Nestled against the S the bent zipper of his jeans had made
In the hollow of his lap.

"A horse is a horse, of corpse, of corpse." He croons softly,
As he lights the flame under the spoon.
He has lost the spoon he used to use.
This is a different one.
A sugar spoon.
With a short handle.
This one gets real hot,
Real fast,
Sometimes burning the tips of his fingers.
But he is used to it.
He has built calluses on these fingers,
And around the bounds of his tortured soul.

"Get off your high horse!"
He used to hear them say
When he, in truth, would try,
And yet his daily trials were not enough.
They washed their hands of him, for
What is truth?

His laughter wracks his body now,
Still wedged between
The wall and the door.
"I'm getting off on my high horse now."
He yells into the empty night
 In a mock reply
To no one.

As he squirms around his red brick cell
To find a comfortable position,
The plastic syringe
Rolls lazily off his lap
And clatters onto the damp cement below.

"Kiss it up to God." He mumbles,
Fumbling between his legs until he locates the elusive tool.
Trapping it between his fingers, he lifts it up to his face.
His lips meet its thin silver shaft.
"Kiss it up to God." He says again as he aims its sharp tip
At the blotched bruises of his arm,
A long track of hurts that leads down
The purple avenue to his heart.
The silver tip pierces the surface of his sallow skin
And,
With a push of his thumb on the plunger,
The sleek white horse is released from its stall,
Brakes its reins,
Then
Gallops uncontrolled through the blueness of his veins.

His brown eyes slowly close in mute consent,
His body slackens in a heap
As he feels a cold wind blow
Snowflakes through his chestnut mane.

He barely notices
As the great white horse jumps gracefully over the split rail
    fence
And into the unknown field beyond.
He throws his thin arms wide,
Face to the clouds,
Prepared now
For the ride of his life,
And realizing,
Ever so slowly,
He will soon be home for his birthday.

THE EATER OF DREAMS

> *"Look on my works ... and despair!"*
> ~~Ozymandias, Percy Bysshe Shelley

I met a traveler from a southern land
Who said: Two trunk-less legs of human flesh
Were tossed askew across a slope of sand.
Between the rusty rails, on wooden ties,
A human torso rests, now cleft in half
And on the other side, a shattered visage lies,
Whose frozen frown, whose vacant skyward gaze,
Tell of a boy whose passions yet survive—
The Dream that mocked him and the heart that bled.
No pedestal nor plaque there now declares:
"I am The Beast, the Eater of All Dreams!"
Nothing besides the remains. Round the decay
Of that so human wreck, bloody and bare,
The rusty metal tracks stretch far away.

ROSE GARDEN

Bleached white bones,
  jagged,
  sharp-edged,
Point like boney fingers,
  ribs,
  claws,
Paw dry soil
In fruitless effort
  to escape
  their timeless shame,
Their buried fate.

Barren bits of lime,
  point to
  their crime,
The failure of their task
  to guard
  their charge,
  their mollusk meat,
  stolen
To feed the need
  to survive.

I dig now
  deep,
  deeper.
The metal of my shovel tip
  hits grit,
  scoops sand, and
Their buried bones,
A treasure trove of shell

In their earthen grave,
so wide,
so deep,
Forever keeping me
from my dreams
of roses.

THE KILL

Your children are not your children.
They are the sons and daughters of Life's longing for itself.
~~***The Prophet*** *(Kahlil Gibran)*

They held him up,
Like a prized catch,
A trout, perhaps,
His mouth agape,
Gripped by his brown curls,
Face turned toward the camera.
They took turns,
Posed with him
Naked,
His pale flesh
Exposed
To the unforgiving sun.

Once he was Gul Mudin,
His father's fifteen year old
Afghan rose.
Now, he's a statistic,
Bravo Company "kill."

Medic shears severed his pinky finger,
The one that would have been

Henna-stained for his wedding day,
Kept now in plastic Ziploc bag
To desiccate,
Proud trophy—
Wage of war.

IX CASIDA OF THE DARK DOVES
Federico García Lorca

Through the laurel branches
I saw two dark doves.
One was the sun,
The other, the moon.
"Little neighbor," I said,
"Where is my grave?"
"In my tail," said the sun.
"In my throat," said the moon.
And, as I was walking
With the earth around my waist,
I saw two snow eagles.
And a naked girl:
One was the other,
And the girl was none.
"Eaglettes," I said.
"Where is my grave?"
"In my tail," said the sun.
"In my throat," said the moon.
Through the laurel branches,
I saw two naked doves:
One was the other,
And both of them were none.

Translated by Christopher Bogart

MY BOHEMIAN LIFE
Arthur Rimbaud

I set off, fists stuffed into torn pockets,
My overcoat too was becoming idyllic.
I was under the sky, Oh Muse! And I was your slave.
Oh! Of what splendid loves I dreamed!

My only pair of pants bore a huge hole.
Tom Thumb dreamer, I released rhymes along my way,
Sought shelter in the Great Bear.
In the night sky, my stars sweetly glimmered.

And, sitting by the roadside, I listened to them
On beautiful September evenings, I felt drops
Of dew, like potent wine, on my forehead.

There, rhyming in the middle of fantastical shadows,
I plucked the shoestrings of my tattered boots
As if they were strings on a lyre—a foot closer to my heart.

Translated by Christopher Bogart

THE CONVERSATION

The room is empty. The walls have been given one thin coat of green wash, each broad brushstroke creating a subtle patch quilt of various shades. Pitted, unvarnished wood planks make up the floor. We sit on simple grey metal folding chairs in the center of the room, facing each other. However, the décor, or lack of it, is irrelevant. The presence of the fifteen year old Hondureño is the only thing that matters, for this conversation will determine who he will become, or whether he will even survive.

His physical stature and appearance are not what you would expect for someone his age, his growth stunted by hunger no doubt, his body dressed in a filthy pair of black jeans with a clothesline belt. A threadbare tee shirt, smudged with dirt and grime, hangs loosely off brown shoulders. A shock of black curly hair tangles in a war for placement above his feral gaze. His bare feet dangle, barely meeting the floor. Dark soil has accumulated under the nails of his fingers and his toes. A beaten up soiled canvas backpack rests by the side of his chair.

I break the silence.

"Hello, Pollo. How are you today?"

Hola. His somewhat hoarse voice has a hint of hesitation. *Muy bien.*

"Your name is Pollo, isn't it?"

Sí. Es lo que me llaman, he responds cautiously. "That's what they call me."

"Why do they call you that?" I ask, even though I already know the answer.

"Because I like chicken. And I'm good at finding it."

"Where do you find the chicken?" My delivery sounds almost too elementary for a fifteen-year-old boy. However, even though I know his age, appearances can be deceptive.

"At the *basurero municipal*, the village dump."

"The village dump? In what village?"

"San Jerónimo Emiliani."

I know all of his answers before he gives them. It is his intonation that I'm looking for, and what questions and responses will unlock his emotions. I want to find out more about him. So I keep up the game, and let him tell me what he knows. What I already know.

"That's where you come from, isn't it?"

"I guess."

"Don't you know?" I ask in mock curiosity.

"No," he responds, as if he were realizing this for the very first time.

"What's the first thing you remember?"

"I remember meeting Marvin on the town square the day my brother died."

"Your brother Norman?"

"Yeah," he looks a little confused. "Did you know him?"

"I met him once."

"You met him?" Pollo's eyes open wide, clearly surprised by this fact.

"In a manner of speaking."

"What's that mean?"

"I know your brother."

"How?"

"I can't explain it right now." I change the topic quickly. "Tell me about Marvin."

"Did you know Marvin?" Pollo asks, his voice tinged with disbelief.

"You could say that."

"How did you know Marvin?"

"I met him once or twice." I am intentionally evasive. "Why don't you tell me about Marvin."

"He was one of the boys I knew from the town." His voice is cautious now—uncertain.

"Knew?"

"Yeah." He is unable to hide the tinge of sadness that quickly crosses his face. " He's dead now."

I counterfeit shock. "What happened?"

"He was *resistolero. Resistoleros* die."

"What are *resistoleros*?"

Pollo looks at me with steady eyes, old eyes for a boy so young. "Resistol's yellow glue. People call the kids that huff it *resistoleros*. When you huff it, you don't feel so hungry. So alone."

"Are you *resistolero*?" I ask, already knowing the answer.

"No," he responds quickly. "My brother died from it. So did Marvin. I don't want to die."

"What's in the bag?" I change the subject abruptly.

"A book." He pulls the bag around and positions it between his knees, then pulls it open. The zipper has long been broken. He reaches into the backpack and takes out a hardback book with a frayed soiled cloth cover displaying a picture of a knight in silver armor on horseback.

"Your book?" I ask innocently, pointing to the book in his hand.

"Yes." He hesitates. "It used to be Marvin's—but it's mine now."

"Do you read?"

"Yes." He voice betrays a little trepidation. I know he's lying.

"Read something for me." He opens the book to a random page and begins to tell a story. He has a limited vocabulary—stilted, clearly not the vocabulary of the writer. "You're not reading," I say simply.

"Yes I am," his response, aggressive, almost hostile.

"Ok." I reach over calmly and take the book out of his hands. I open the book and find the first page, turn the open book around, then place it back into his hands. "Read this." I point to the first paragraph.

He sits there, silent and sullen.

"You can't read, can you?"

"No."

"Could Marvin read?" I change the subject to save him any further embarrassment.

"He told us he could; but, after a while, I knew he couldn't."

"How did you know?"

"Every time he read us a story, he used different words." He sits silently for a bit, thinking of Marvin. "I didn't care," he says defensively. "He told good stories."

"Do you miss him?"

"Yeah. I guess so." He tightens his grip on the book.

"Is the money still in the binding?" I surprise him by asking this question. He looks up at me.

"How do you know about that?'

"I know about a lot of things." Smug.

Pollo pulls the book closer to his chest, as if I were going to steal it. "Why did Marvin give you the book with the money in it?"

His face clouds over. "He knew he was dying and he wanted to give me the chance to escape this life." He gestures to the window. "He wanted me to have a better life in America." His face now reflects as much pain as he will allow it.

"He must have been a good friend."

"He was like an older brother to me." He thinks a minute. "He was like an older brother to all of us." He stares down at the book in his hands, lost in thought.

Then he looks up at me, suddenly. "How do you know so much about us?"

The time has come to tell him the truth.

"Because I created you."

Pollo's face contorts in disbelief.

"You're my father?"

"No," I answer him quickly, then smile. "Well, maybe. . . in a way." I lean forward, placing my elbows on my knees. "I am a writer. I write stories. And you are one of the characters in one of my stories."

His brow knits as he tries to understand what I have just told him.

"So I'm not real?"

"Oh, you're real. At least here you're real."

He looks even more confused.

"As we have been talking, haven't you wondered how I knew so much about you? About your brother? About Marvin?"

"Yeah. Kind of."

"And haven't you wondered why you have no memories of your life before your brother, Norman, died? Or before you met Marvin?"

He stares at me in silence.

"Do you remember anything about Norman other than the fact that he was your big brother? Do you remember growing up with him? Do you remember your mother or your father?" I pause to let some of this sink in. He sits opposite me, motionless. Still.

"And haven't you asked yourself how you only speak Spanish and I am speaking only English, yet we seem to be able to understand each other?"

"I don't understand." Pollo looks down to his lap, deeply disturbed. "Was any of my life real?"

"All of it was, Pollo. At least the part you remember."

"Is that why I don't remember being a child?"

"Yeah," I tell him. "You only remember the story I wrote about you and Marvin."

"So I didn't exist before I met Marvin?"

"In a way, no. I had to create a back story for you. You know, some background about your childhood. Just no specific events that you would remember."

"Why did you do that?"

"Because I had to establish a life for you before you met Marvin. He saw you, actually, when your brother sent him down to the *basurero municipal*."

He looks up at me. "What was I doing?"

"Doing what you do best—looking for scraps of chicken on discarded fried chicken bones." All of a sudden, I feel ashamed. I feel as if I have used him badly. "Don't you remember?" I ask, somewhat lamely. "That's how you got your name."

Pollo sits there for a while, thinking. Then he suddenly looks up, agitated, and points his index finger at me. "You killed Marvin!"

"Well, yeah. I guess. But only in the story."

"That story was my life! You took away my brother, Norman, then took away Marvin!"

"I had to." I now feel defensive. "That's the way I wrote the story."

"Why did you tell this story," he sneers, "if you had to kill the only two people I cared about? Why did you do that?" He looks at me. I can see the anguish in his eyes. I hadn't expected this. He existed, I had reasoned, only as a character from my imagination. I shouldn't care how he feels, yet here an undernourished miserable fifteen year kid from the village dump sits in front of me—in agony. . . an agony that I caused. I don't feel too good about it.

"You have to understand," I try to explain. "Every story has a moral. Just like the stories Marvin told you."

"Yeah," he acknowledges, "but in Marvin's stories, sometimes the hero won. Marvin was a hero. Why couldn't you have let him win?"

"Pollo," I look into his brown eyes. "Stories are written to be told. Just like Marvin told you all those stories," I point to the book wrapped in his arms, "to teach you lessons. Lessons of bravery, about heroism, about never giving up."

"Then why did you kill him? What did he do to you?" He paused to think. "What did he do wrong?"

"He didn't do anything wrong, Pollo." I pause to think of how I can explain this to him.

"Then why did you kill him?" he insists.

I lean forward again and rest my arms on my knees. "Because sometimes heroes lose. Sometimes heroes die."

"Why?" His voice whines as a child would who refuses to accept reality.

"Because sometimes that is the only thing that they can do to save those they care about."

"How did killing Marvin save us?"

"Because, Pollo, when people read his story they will realize what is happening down here to the homeless children of Central America. They will learn about how grinding poverty condemns people to a life of misery." I stop to let some of what I am saying sink in. "How children sometimes are forced to use Resistol to dull that hunger, that pain. And how the glue kills them, the way it killed Norman. The way it killed Marvin." We both sit in silence as Pollo looks down at Marvin's book again, trying to understand. After a few minutes, he lifts his eyes from his lap.

"What's going to happen to me now? Is the story over?"

"The first story is, yes."

He thinks for a few seconds. "What do you mean the first story?"

"The first story was called 'The Beast'."

"What about the money in the spine of Marvin's book, the money Marvin told me would help me to travel north to seek a better life?" It is now my turn to sit silently and think. "Couldn't that be another story?"

"It could," I admit. "It could." I am playing for time.

"Then why don't you write it?" When I don't answer, he looks at me, his eyes showing signs of dawning understanding. "You already know what my story will be. And how it will end, don't you?" Again, I remain silent. "Don't you?" he insists, cleverly.

"What was the last thing you remember before you were here?"

Pollo stops to think.

"Burying Marvin with Moisés and José Antonio."

I decide to level with him. "That is the first scene of the new story."

"My story?"

"Yes."

"What is it called? Does it have a name?"

"Its title for now is 'The Quest'."

Pollo sits there, trying to take it all in.

"Is this the story about how I travel north to a better life in America?"

"Well, it is part of that story."

"You mean there's another story after that?" Now he is truly interested, forgetting his guarded demeanor and allowing himself to show begrudging interest.

"Yeah. I'm thinking of calling it 'The Grail'."

"*Joder!*" Pollo curses in amazement. "What happens in that story? Do I finally get to America?"

"Listen, Pollo. I can't tell you what is going to happen in these stories. If you know how the story ends, it will change what you do in the story. Don't you think Marvin would have thought twice if he knew that, by standing up on the top of that train, he would fall and lose a leg and end his life as *resistolero*?" I hesitate. "Besides, I'm not even sure that I am going to write these stories."

"You're not going to write the stories?" His voice rises in indignation. "Why not?"

"I have already planned these stories out. I know what will happen to you in both stories. I don't know whether, particularly now since I've met you and gotten to know you, I want you to go through the suffering that lies ahead of you."

"You created me. You put me through all this. You owe me," he says slowly, deliberately. " Don't you think you should give me the chance to at least try?"

"You don't know what's ahead for you, Pollo. It will be difficult. Very difficult"

"And living from day to day, dressed in rags, always dirty, hungry, combing through mounds of garbage to find a scrap of food or clothing isn't difficult? At least if you let me try to find out whether I have a chance at a better life, I will have the one thing that I don't have now."

"What is that?"

"Hope."

I am amazed at the crude eloquence of this feral child.

"You created Marvin. Through the stories of knights in shining armor that he told us, we began to believe for the first time that it might just get better for us one day. You said that you killed Marvin so that people would know what it was like for us. Marvin killed himself so that I could have the chance he blew." He looks directly into my eyes. "You wrote that story. Won't you give me the chance you sacrificed Marvin for?" He stands, places Marvin's book into his canvas bag, and slings the bag over his shoulder.

"You created me. Won't you give me the same chance that you gave Marvin?"

I look down at my hands. There seems nothing more to say. I think about what I know of the life that lies ahead of him, and the dangers that it will entail. For the first time in this whole time, I realize that I have feelings for this character I have created. In a way, he wasn't that far off when he asked me whether I was his father. I can still hear the repressed yearning in his voice—the kid who desperately wants to know where he comes from, and if he is loved. I dread sending him out on this journey. I know what challenges he will have to face before he completes his quest. That one day, he too will be a writer—and that it is through me that his story will be told. I am feeling the beginnings of what feels like parental pride for this boy I bore from the garbage heap. I want to hug him before he goes. I want to tell him to be brave. That I am proud of him. Even though, deep down, he probably wants it, he is much too tough for a hug. That's ok. He will need that toughness for what lies ahead.

I raise my head to stand, to look at him one more time and, at least, to shake his hand. His chair is empty. In the far off distance, I hear the faint whistle of a freight train.

VISIT TO VERONA

Over the many years that I have been visiting her, my Aunt Edie and I have developed certain traditions. Nothing fancy. Simple traditions. Like the lunch she makes when I arrive in her apartment. Or the walk we take in Verona Park. Dinner at Meile's or the Caldwell Diner. Or Linda's Chicken. Most often at Linda's. We have at times varied this itinerary over the years with shopping trips into Montclair or the Verona Arts and Crafts Fair or Eagle Rock State Park. But mostly, it is lunch in the apartment, a walk in Verona Park, and dinner at Linda's Chicken. "Chris," she says with a big grin on her face as if she is hiding a secret like maybe she won the million-dollar lottery. "They have creamed spinach today!" In all honesty, their creamed spinach is delicious. Spiced and creamed just right. And their chicken! Cooked over an open fire until it is crispy yet juicy. Their side orders, like the acorn squash or their smashed potatoes, are equally mouth watering. But it isn't just Linda's Chicken or Verona Park that brings me up to the mountains far too infrequently. It is my Aunt Edie.

My aunt and I are not even really blood related. She and my Uncle Sey were friends of my father and mother before I was born. I was born and raised a Roman Catholic in Queens, sent to Catholic grammar school, Catholic high school and a Catholic college. My Aunt Edie is Jewish, from Polish Jewish stock who immigrated to Brooklyn at the turn of the century— the last one, that is. But over the years of shared laughter, shared conversation, shared loss and shared joy, she and I have become *mishpocheh*. Family.

And well she should be. She has been a constant presence in my life and in my memory. Through old black and white pictures, I have a continuum of images of her—the beautiful young raven-haired woman of my youth, sitting on a blanket in the park, her tresses cascading down her back to the wise little elf with the pixie haircut, the same color in her seventies as the woman in the park of my youth. Her face still retains that same guileless innocence; her eyes, that same twinkle of mischief and mirth. It is as if she has not passed a single day since the first day I met her, for the lines of age in her face merely underline the virtues already present and comfortable in her nature. And the awe I have always had of her, the mystery that has surrounded many raven-haired beauties of history, surrounds her still. On the day my father had taken me for my first haircut as a very little boy, I lifted my head from my tears to see a picture on the calendar hanging on the wall in the barbershop of a dark-haired young woman sitting on a blanket, her long dark tresses flowing over her naked shoulders, her scarlet lips in a pout. "Look!" I cried out with glee, pointing to the calendar on the wall. "Aunt Edie!"

My aunt was a child of the Great Depression, much like my mother was; and, like all children born during a time when money and jobs were scarce, they learned certain lessons about life. Just not the same lessons. My mother, like other children that had experienced the Depression, came to adulthood swearing that their children would never live the way they had. As a result, my generation struggles with excess weight given us by our parents in an effort to be sure we were never hungry. When my family had company, let's say four or five visitors, there was food on the table for twenty. I don't know whether they did it because they could or because they wanted people to believe they could. Whatever the reason, it had the same result—the support of a thriving health and fitness industry from fad diets, "great abs," exercise programs and exercise equipment that can be folded up and shoved under the bed when not in use. But that's not the lesson my aunt learned from the Great Depression.

Frugality. That's what my aunt learned from the Great Depression. And she learned it the hard way. She grew up in New York City at a time when immigrant families got by on the barest of necessities. She has told me of stuffing cardboard into old shoes to cover the holes in the soles, of wearing two and three summer-weight hand-me-down jackets in snow as a substitute for a winter coat, and of looking at clothing as functional not in a stylistic sense, but as practical necessity. She and her brothers and sisters learned at an early age to become smart shoppers, not by comparing prices to look for the best buys, but when her family was unable to pay their tab at the neighborhood store, of finding different food merchants that did not know them and would offer them the credit that they desperately needed to eat and survive. Toys were whatever discarded items were available. An empty carton or wooden crate. A broken and discarded baby carriage. With a little imagination, these could be transformed into an escape from the barren streets of the city, and the drab bare existence they represented. It was these ghosts that taught valuable lessons in the frailty of human existence, lessons not soon forgotten.

I was sitting at her kitchen table on one of my most recent visits, watching her make my sandwich. She laid the small leaves of lettuce on the roll as though she was laying a newborn infant into a crib. And as I watched the care with which she handled the very food that we would be devouring in a matter of minutes, I realized the deep respect she had for this necessity of life. It reminded me of one time when she had come to my house for dinner, and was watching me clean up after the meal. "What are you doing with that?" she had asked me.

"With what?" I asked, almost unaware that I was doing anything special.

"With that broccoli."

What broccoli, I thought. There was only one stalk left in the bowl. "I don't know," I responded, somewhat confused. "Throwing it away?"

"Don't throw it away," she said, gently but firmly. "There are people in the world that would kill for that food."

I looked down at the stalk of broccoli dumbly. "What am I going to do with it?"

"Put it in a little plastic wrap and put it in the fridge."

"For what?" I asked, still not getting it.

"You can put it salad tomorrow for lunch. With a little oil and vinegar." I looked into her face, and saw an expression that was trying to convince me of the reasonableness of the suggestion. And of its importance to her.

And as I watched her in her own kitchen spreading the tuna salad on the lettuce, I was further reminded of the importance that food had in her early life. And to the lengths she had to go to insure its continued presence to her family in her childhood. She placed two slices of tomato on each sandwich, and then wrapped the half tomato remaining in plastic wrap and placed it in the fridge. The images of childhood can be a great consolation in adulthood; and the ghosts of childhood can teach frightening and unforgettable lessons.

And while my aunt still values the importance of frugality as a virtue, she also values generosity as a virtue of equal importance. The juxtaposition of these two virtues have sometimes confused me, but always taught me how complex and yet wonderful her character is, and how gracefully she wears it. I called her one August day a few years ago, and, in conversation, mentioned that I had been at the beach and found a ten-dollar bill on the sand at the water's edge, snagged in a piece of old fishing netting.

"Put it in the bank," she stated unequivocally.

"Why?" I asked out of curiosity. (Sometimes I wonder whether I ever learn.)

"Found money makes money. Put it in the bank and it will make you more money."

What did I have to lose? So the following day I went to the bank and deposited the faded ten-dollar bill in my savings account. The following afternoon when the mail arrived, I noticed a card from my aunt. Inside it read, "Thinking of you. Love, Aunt Edie." And in the card was a check for one thousand dollars.

I called my aunt. "What's this all about?"

"Uncle Sey and I were talking and we decided that we'd like to give you some money so that you don't have to wait for us to die to enjoy it. This way we'll be alive to see you enjoy it."

"That's not necessary," I said, a little embarrassed by the generosity of the gift.

"I know it's not necessary" was her quick response. "It's something we wanted to do. That's all."

"Ok," I said contritely. "Thank you."

"You're welcome," she responded simply. There was a brief moment of silence as I tried to think of something more original to say. But she beat me to the punch.

"See. I told you found money makes money." I could almost see the twinkle in her eye over the phone lines. She had gotten me. "Put it in the bank," she added. "It will be part of the down payment on a house one day."

She was right. That thousand dollars was the beginning of a drive to save and bank over the following two years. And in August, just two years after I had found that ten-dollar bill, I bought my house.

"You ready to go?" my aunt asks me as she rinses the lunch dishes in the kitchen sink. "Sure," I respond, and we leave the apartment and walk down Springfield Avenue toward Verona Park. "I want to stop at the Luncheonette and get a lottery ticket" she comments to me as we stride down Springfield Avenue, her two steps to every one of mine. Sometimes we stop at the pharmacy to see what new sales they are having. And sometimes we walk to her bank if she needs to do some quick transaction. The first day we went to the bank on one of our walks, she was just recovering from one of the many illnesses that my aunt has had to cope with in her life. I was concerned about her ability to handle quite such a long walk so soon into her recovery. I didn't really know how to slip into the conversation that maybe driving to the bank might be in her better interests. "Where is this bank?" I asked as subtly as I could.

"Don't worry," she responded. "You'll recognize it by the flag that flies out in front of it."

"Flag?" I asked, not sure of what she was trying to tell me.

"Yeah. Flag," she said, with a slight touch of annoyance. "The one with the money sign on it." Ok. Now you don't have to hit me with a bat. She's up to the walk and my best strategy is to drop it. The flag with the money sign. Good one, Aunt Edie!

But today we are not going to deposit money. Today we have a mission. Today we are going to spend it. "I didn't know you bought lottery tickets," I commented to her, a little surprised that my aunt would participate in anything that akin to gambling. As if I were the representative from the country of Frugality.

"It's 92 million dollars today," she says.

"You know," I comment, trying subtly to inject a note of fiscal reality into the conversation, and finding it hard to believe that I am the one doing it. "They say that you have a better chance of being struck by lightning than by winning the lottery."

"Never know unless you try," she says as we enter the store. "You buy one too. It's only a dollar." We purchase our tickets and are filling them out on top of a pile of newspapers.

"You have a system?" I ask.

"Sure," she replies. "*Ickel-michel.*"

Now I know about the famous *ickel-michel.* I've seen my aunt find us parking spaces, good bargains, and good seats in the park all by *ickel-mickel.* But now she was going to use it to win a large sum of money.

I used to think, when I heard her use the expression, that it was Yiddish. My aunt was forever trying to teach me Yiddish. Her conversations were peppered with it. Sometimes to listen to her talk she sounded as if she were speaking "y'english". So when I first heard this expression, I ran to my copy of Rosten's **The Joys of Yiddish**. No luck. So I called her on the phone. "Aunt Edie. I can't find *ickel-mickel* in the Yiddish book."

"That's because it's not Yiddish."

"What is it?" I ask curiously.

"Nothing. It's like *Snickelfritz und Frautzen*. I made it up."

"You made up Snickelfritz and Frautzen!" I exclaimed incredulously. Now I remember my Uncle Sey telling me once that his family belonged to a Native American tribe. The Shmedrick Indians. That was funny! My Uncle Sey had a dry wit that never failed to hit the mark. He explained to me once that when he died, he would be buried in the family plot in the Jewish cemetery in Brooklyn. "You know" he told me, "your aunt is not going to be with me." Surprised, I asked where she was going to be buried. "Your aunt wants to be cremated, and her ashes spread over Long Pond Lake. I am still going to have her name engraved next to mine on the tombstone. But instead of her dates below her name, I am just going to put *nickt du*. Not here." That was my uncle's sense of humor. But that the steadfast Snickelfritz and the loyal but slightly insane Frautzen were made up was just too much to believe. My aunt used to come over to our home in Canarsie when I was a boy of four and babysat when my parents went out. I used to look forward to those times for days in advance. She would bring me a little cardboard box that looked not unlike a little valise filled with Anne Morris fruit lollypops. We would sit on the couch with the yellow slipcovers adorned with large rose colored floral prints, and she would regale me with stories of the adventures of Snickelfritz and Frautzen. I had always thought they were real, and that if I could slip into their world, what larks we would have!

"So you are going to use *ickel-mickel*," I respond, in the pharmacy, looking over at her.

"Sure. Aren't you?"

"Of course," I responded with a smile, and we gave the man at the counter our tickets and our money and left the store.

"What are you going to do with the money if you win?" she asks, like it was a sure thing.

"I am going to send you back to visit Israel."

"Oh no," she replies. "I can't do that now. Maybe another time." And we stroll across the street and into Verona Park.

We spent that afternoon, as we had on every visit, talking of the latest news of friends and relatives, remembering stories from our shared past, and talking about the future, mostly mine. We spoke of the alien face that appeared like magic on the bottom of an old frying pan, or one of her "past lives" as a young Chinese girl in a country town in the Chinese provinces. There was a certain feeling of safety and predictability about her life. And like a huge bubble, one in which she gathered everyone that was near her. And we felt safe, warm and loved just being near her. And her future seemed to be as preordained as the continuous stream of todays she lived every day. She liked her life, and those of us who are lucky enough to share a small part of it with her, liked it too.

Later, we went to Linda's Chicken for dinner. They had creamed spinach.

Emanuel di Pasquale

LOOSE HORSE

Unbridled, clean of all harness,
it swings on its back legs,
almost dances, snorts
and daintily shakes its mane—
unattended, his own beast.

MEETING

I return from a walk
along a dirt road
and meet my footsteps.
The trees keep their secrets.

Stephen Dunn

POEM FOR PEOPLE WHO ARE UNDERSTANDABLY TOO BUSY TO READ POETRY

Relax. This won't last long.
Or if it does, or if the lines
make you sleepy or bored,
give in to sleep, turn on
the T.V., deal the cards.
This poem is built to withstand
such things. Its feelings
cannot be hurt. They exist
somewhere in the poet,
and I am far away.
Pick it up anytime. Start it
in the middle if you wish.
It is as approachable as melodrama,
and can offer you violence
if it is violence you like. Look,
there's a man on a sidewalk;
the way his leg is quivering
he'll never be the same again.
This is your poem
and I know you're busy at the office
or the kids are into your last nerve.
Maybe it's sex you've always wanted.
Well, they lie together
like the party's unbuttoned coats,
slumped on the bed
waiting for drunken arms to move them.
I don't think you want me to go on;
everyone has his expectations, but this
is a poem for the entire family.
Right now, Budweiser

is dripping from a waterfall,
deodorants are hissing into armpits
of people you resemble,
and the two lovers are dressing now,
saying farewell.
I don't know what music this poem
can come up with, but clearly
it's needed. For it's apparent
they will never see each other again
and we need music for this
because there was never music when he or she
left you standing on the corner.
You see, I want this poem to be nicer
than life. I want you to look at it
when anxiety zigzags your stomach
and the last tranquilizer is gone
and you need someone to tell you
I'll be here when you want me
like the sound inside a shell.
The poem is saying that to you now.
But don't give anything for this poem.
It doesn't expect much. It will never say more
than listening can explain.
Just keep it in your attache case
or in your house. And if you're not asleep
by now, or bored beyond sense,
the poem wants you to laugh. Laugh at
yourself, laugh at this poem, at all poetry.
Come on:

Good. Now here's what poetry can do.

Imagine yourself a caterpillar.
There's an awful shrug and, suddenly,
you're beautiful for as long as you live.

Melissa Febos

CHAMBERMAID

I shuffle across the courtyard with my plastic bin of cleaning supplies, past the pool where sun-drunk children with popsicle-stained mouths scream in the shallow end. On the concrete patio, women squint at each other's bodies, consulting their husbands' shoulders with viscous lotions. Their husbands appraise my new body. The feeling of being young is only enjoyed in retrospect; I always feel older than I did before. Desire, mine, not mine, moors me to an action. The men see, and I feel, the jostle of the bin against my hip, the t-shirt riding up my waist, the muscular shifts in my thighs as I crouch to pick up a discarded wrapper. At home, after the boys whom I sneak into my bedroom sneak back out, I trace the path their hands took across my body.

The day after my fourteenth birthday, my father took me to the Town Hall to get my work permit. My future whispers with the flutter of checkbooks, passports, licenses, tax returns, and invoices. The smell of adulthood is the smell of paper, as mysterious and sure as that of any book.

Who doesn't know how to clean, I think. I've been doing my own laundry since I was ten. But there are tricks to learn, things *that people notice,* Brandy, my boss with the sun-baked face informs me. There are light bulbs to swipe with a rag. There are paper seals to affix to toilet seats, to assure guests of their sanitation, *no one else's ass has ever sat here* these papers falsely promise. There is Windex to be liberally sprayed into the silent air conditioners, so that when they moan to life, they exhale the smell of clean.

The Sleepy Hollow Inn is near the beach, but it is for those tourists without a house in town, who can't afford the B&B's with manicured gardens, dowager mistresses, and historic molding over their porches. These are the tourists with too many children, who speak too loudly in restaurants, who walk down our Cape Cod streets wearing Cape Cod T-shirts, mouth full of salt-water taffy. The rich are also gross, though crueler, as I will discover in the restaurants that occupy the rest of my summers here. For now, it is these people's stained sheets that I will strip from the beds with rubber gloves and wash in load after load after load. It is their crumpled panties and yellowed condoms that I will empty from the wicker trash baskets and fish out from under the beds with a broom handle. It is their menses, urine, saliva, and hair that I will wipe from the bathroom floors, the sinks, showers, and toilets, their pus I will scrape from the mirrors.

There is a note of glee in their piggishness, a delight in the freedom anonymity affords. It is impossible that all of their homes are treated this way. They are settling a score. I know that their punishment is not meant for me. The other chambermaids do not have the freedom to quit, as I do; they have babies and overdue phone bills, they have south shore accents and lips lined in brown pencil. They have boyfriends with court dates, cars with no air conditioning, fingernails that click together as they load sheets into the industrial dryers.

My favorite is Jenny. Jenny has a grown out perm, a baby, and eyes that fill half her face. I watch her twist the twine of her hair into a knot atop her head like a magic trick. I love watching her; every movement along some worn groove. The way she pulls a cigarette out of its bright green pack and tucks it between her lips; her slender hands striking matches, folding towels, popping the tab on a can of diet soda. On the hottest days, she ties her shirt ends together to bare her flat stomach, ghosted stretch marks like the skids of a pencil eraser. She pokes her skinny chest out and struts the balconies until Brandy comes out of the office and glowers across the pool. Brandy will never fire Jenny, as she will me. And Jenny will never leave this town.

It is vile work, but the torture is the tedium. In a given day I have twelve rooms to clean, and as many hours as it takes to do so. The other maids linger in the basement, getting paid by the hour to sneak cigarettes and speculate on Brandy's sex life, as they press their soles against the cool cement. They watch television in the rooms with the sound turned down. They shake their heads as I leave after a handful of hours, Brandy frowning at my hastily vacuumed carpets. I have never known boredom like this. I did not know that interesting was a privilege.

Then I find the dress. It hangs in the closet of one of the balcony rooms, a blue, sequined thing. My mother does not own things like this. She doesn't wear the kind of heels that sit below the dress, the feet of some invisible woman. My mother wears sturdy cotton bras and panties, never stockings like those in the particleboard bureau drawers.

I slip the cool skin of that dress over mine, and then there is no line. Their privacy has always been at my discretion. I wear their clothes, spritz my body with their perfumes, shake my head to see their jewelry sparkle in the smeared mirrors. I touch my own body with the imagined hands of their husbands, with the cigarette-thin fingers of Jenny. I twist myself atop their dirty sheets, and pocket a pair of lace panties with a tiny plastic pearl sewn onto the waist.

Although my compulsion grows, my cleaning efficiency does not. Instead of a hastily poor job, I offer a languorously poor one. I am costing Brandy money, she says, on the day that she fires me. I am relieved. I never return my skeleton key. For years after, instead of sneaking my young lovers into my mother's house, I bring them here. I lead them through the shadowy rooms by hand, toward the moonlit beds, beyond which, through the parted curtains, that pool glows, tossing its silvery rays against the concrete walls.

Frank Finale

WORM

Glistening in soil, your body forms
a backward "S" swollen with curves.
You have more hearts than a lark, but no one
hears you sing; the gravel in your gizzard
is a hard note to take. Blindly casting,
you enrich the soil leaving it
holier than before. A knot of energy,
you lure the fish from its school, disgust
the pigtailed girls. With more lives than a cat,
under a child's stick, you go your separate ways.
Rings of your dead dimple an April
puddle. Under it all, you move the earth
straining to receive a dark communion.

Gregg Glory [Gregg G. Brown]

Gregg Glory [Gregg G. Brown] has devoted his life to poetry since happening across a haiku by Moritake, to wit:

> *Leaves*
> *float back up to the branch—*
> *Ah! butterflies.*

He runs the micro-publishing house BLAST PRESS, which has published over two dozen authors in the past 25 years. Named in honor of the wild Vorticist venture by Ezra Pound and Wyndham Lewis, BLAST PRESS is forward-looking and very opinionated.

He still composes poems on his departed father's clipboard, which he's had since High School.

Published in, among other places: *BlueLINE, Exquisite Corpse, Blunderbuss, Monmouth Review, Middlesex: A Literary Journal, Asbury Park Press* (60K circulation). In two NJ anthologies: *Howl of Sorrow: poems about Hurricane Sandy,* and *Palisades, Parkways & Pinelands.*

Co-Host of the long-running River Read Reading Series in Red Bank, which features NJ and national poets.

Associate Editor of the literary magazine *This Broken Shore.* Two-time Asbury Park Poet Laureate awarded by the Asbury Music Awards.

Website: gregglory.com

THE POET TO HIS COUNTRYMEN

Inspiration's a silver ribbon of mist
Fallen thin from high Bridalveil;
Only a whim so cloud-soft can twist
Reality out of the high-fantastical.
Real life begins in utter dream;
In utter dream our rebel rhyme began,
The fought-for fairytale of freedom,
Cloud-soft as the dreaming cheek of woman.

Cloud-soft as a woman's dreaming cheek,
Jefferson's quill spelled out the wild desire;
Soft breath blew dry the shimmering ink
That tossed the regal tyrant to the fire.
Who would dream with me by the fireside
When the great gleeds glimmer and dim
First must soften his headstrong pride
And open his heart to the fire's whim.

Come dream beside me by the gentle fire
That roared old monarchs to the brink;
Come watch the red and yellow-red fire
Until our heads must nod and blink.
Softly, softly silver inspiration's mist
Flies chiming from high Bridalveil peak;
Listen to what whispering winds insist,
Cloud-soft as dreaming woman's cheek.

ASCENT

Awake, awake!
For all the dear bay's glistening
In uneven light still listening
For whatever of utterance
Soul's chrysolm beauty may glance
Into willing water's dark,
My sweet meaning the whole of my bark.

Set sail, set sail, my soul, set sail
Let no hindrance, no halt, avail:
For we are the sweet of the tree,
Blossom and bole, shoot and root we three:
Myself, my soul, and me.

Nor does the shaping heart forego
To lend its beat to our argot--
My spirit a crystalline keel,
Inspiration a motion wind feels
Lifting in blessing ascent
All some deeper sleep had blent
With nightmare chimeras now forgot
By all within my steady boat.

Every morning wayfarer
Whose light boat cannot tarry—
Pushes on out of darkness
With whatever of best and best
In tangles of light impressed
In bossing golds on waves' breast
Plies resistless to the crest!

Out of the sullen east the sun
Has given my soul a tongue:

From here commences, in my sight,
An headlong, eternal light
That every living form bedights—
From the gentle fount of grass
To the living wave like glass
No such light may overpass
But must ignite in simpleness
Love's million multiple beams!

Such silver as the eglantine
To dew-fraught morn resigns
And heaven on every still thing deigns
Rewarding quiet prayers
With this mercurial layer—
Such silver I say is savior!

When soul its own good blossom knows
Nor will be shaken by the cold
Into something hard and old
A sheath of clear protecting
Such firm flowers thus selecting
Deep winter's dire infecting
Shall not break them by its cold,
Such clear light protecting.

All last night my heart had lain
Upon this boat and silver stream
Until all memory became
Like the memory of a dream;
And there true life began—
Beneath night's stars swirled to one
Past the extinguishment of suns
When realer dream draws us on
To dream of all we may have been
And in heart's solace draws us on
In dreaming dream to dream again!

I my own bright soul create
Nor did this fascination make
To slave it to a universe
I, living, gaze on as a hearse.
My silver hand in dawn's lake
Dips, its own soul to take;
From this sweet enlivening
Come my symbols unquestioning:
Crown upon my crown rests cherishing,
The sword in my hand unperishing.

Do not dispraise the light
That, singing whatever's brightest,
Undoes the theft of night—
In soul-enchanting soliloquies
Enmansioning aerial ways
That we might thrive there all our days
In realms of spendless purity
Absent nations' perfidy
Heart to heart for sole surety:

This our pledge, this our guarantee
That all's well with humanity
Once these bleak constants, fear and dread,
Lay to light exposed, and dead,
The human plant may only mend,
Think to create, and speak to praise,
Throughout the endless paradise of days
—Touch to caress, or move to love,
As this thoughtless rhyme does prove.

Whatever slender wing endeavors
Be communicant with the treasure
One heart may hold forever
Will find such wind in chambers there

Beyond conjoining woe or care
That they may sail infinity
In the air of that one heart's ease.
Pleasure alone may live within
The human bound of life given
As light within these waters:
Ungrieving, crystalline, faultless.

Read at Pier Village Poetry Festival, July 4th, 2016

THE JENNY WREN

The jenny wren for what she is is not
Lauded, though her song's long remembered
Even unto the stretching-out of night
When completed day to partial dream's transferred:
All I'd sensed as simple in August light
Returns entangled as a promise half-recalled.
How had I missed her among the spurring dusts?
Who'd hopped unnoted from spot to spot
As dawn unbed me to my daily ends?
This fussless singing miss whose flipped tail tilts
To say nothing's so fine as front-yard friends?
Evening stillness finds me failing, half-appalled
At all I'd left undone to which I did accede,
Awaiting dream remembrance of the wren I need.

FALSIFYING FIRE

Our sullen retreat into the ever-there,
Our reliance on the invisible
Or recourse to given revelation,
Brightens my minute's thought to crucible
And pulls some lasting gold from my flame's care,
As if we knew our wishing and the wish were one.
What do we need of what seems infinite?
The partial glare of being here, just here,
Is enough of heaven to round our minute
And puts a light, however lone and bare
We cry for things more determinate,
Into all we seem to see and share.
I will not falsify my fire, but answer all and one:
No answer yet but becoming to become.

BY SHADOW KNOWN

I did not know how clouds could crowd
The weathered Earth by blowing round,
Or drop deep shadows by their light,
Too much lightness in sun's too much light.

'Til one day their dark put me dark—
Crowded me out by high-shadowed marks
From old communion with the sun;
Daily now my darkness comes.

I, who had been a burning cloud,
Now in noon-night perform my rounds.
Were I to shred their silver dark,
New light would blind by being stark.

DISSEMBLING SEMBLANCE

Lie there, my art —*Prospero*

1

Ho-ho!   From out his party grave, up-popped
The skeletal self that Tenor'd tamed.
Dewy longings drift half-wet, in ziggurats,
Down the dirty sticks of his dry fact,
Lending a silver-inlay to his polar bones.
Desire sniffs for roses through groutless nose-holes
And musty wines slalom a gorgeless gob.
Nothing of the lover, of the brother
Lingers here.   I stick four mournful fingers
Through his clackers for a tongue, wagging
Idiot digits in mime Shakespearean.
No Yasunarian voice, Horatio, ensued.
No Ophelian sonnets rained in daisy-chains.
Lipless ivories inferred infernal grins.
Tongueless Tenor Semblance, disinterred,
Master-man and mirror-me, was DEAD!   And I?

2

I am no Poet-Frankenstein, evoking souls
From wounded earth.   For me, a hole is a hole
Is a hole.   Love caressed, love cupped, love cuffed
Suckles living teats, not this bony xylophone.
Still, I loiter here half-longingly and toe
Pale parabolas of a pelvis furred with mold.
I, too, shall one day come undone, un-
Buttoned before the mawkish gawkers in the wood,
Dining on no niceties but dusty praise.
And you, and you.   Bluets brush my boots,
Sans author in penless processional.
Tallied Tenor here, pure loss, is less and less,—
A condensate escaped in Gobi air.

What last farewell, or goodbye cry, can I
Cachinnate for such luckless kin?
Feral fate! The day, the hour, is late.

3

Though crass and cursed and cloistered
In a hole, my man of clay, who I made,
Unmade me. Iffy gift! Solitude still knows:
To live our lithest days in sackcloth is a sin.
My vampire mirror blings, bingeing on blanks.
I miss the mischievous elf I myself had minted,
Wry coinage of a brain love-benumbed.
Impresario of puppets, piccolo fish
Waving in a world wigged with sideways seagrass,
I command my scarecrow scalawag, Tenor
(Whom I marched off to death, alas) a last
Resurrection reappearance imagineer.
Coffin-lid, crack! Earth erupt and burp-up
Voodoo me, vanished voice and vair ermine.
Pffft! And see, through misty mazy day,
In his water-wings and goggle-gear. . . .

4

"Irksome apparition! Clavicle and skull
But prank the picked-out polychromes of life
More sullied dull. Pink is less pricked than pinky.
How can twanged canaries out-crow sepulchers?
Muddy mausoleums high-rise our tipping tropes.
No quip out-kids a skeleton's ghastly grin."
So I solemnized in my preacher's best.
But cut-rate Tenor in his rotted tux
Retailed another fable, made gritty
By eternal Time's half-sandy clasp.
"Birds of paradise in their jungle mung
Whistle fluent waltzes more queer than square.
When kisses come twitting 'tween the stars,

Their ache is more than mausoleums are.
The softest-rose of live lips out-quips
Clown-corpse midgets and their brazen cars. The curds
Of life are sacred, but only as we sip."

5

So I sat in puzzlement complete.
Head-hanging, feet-dangling, I weeped. I kicked
Spic hobnails against the grave's gouged walls.
I did not want to hum, or ham, the mournful measure
A mealy mouth had found. Must I have more to say?
To do, to be? Was wishing up to me?
Argent star and pentecostal ghost! It was.
The prolog past was mere evaporate *because.*
I zipped upon the slipping ice, slouch-hatted,
As I myself alone, floe to floe.

Tenor was my made-up man, my solo ghost;
Of his fragile form, I was holy host.
Vital tailor! Sledding immortality but slips
Us in our heart-stitched skins again.
Thus we see, beyond Death's batty beam,
Is is brighter than the vim of seems.

6

How, in all this claustric Ought, ought I
To utter and confess my consummate
"Ow to Joy"? Life is pain, and fidgets
As it sings. Dr. Formaldehyde in his lab-coat,
Peering in, thumbs an icy stethoscope to quiz
All coughs, all crimes. What Rabelaisian
Parable am I in? What sly reply does this
Inquisitive pin in my inflated thigh
Giggle to confide? None, none.
All my splendid spillages funnel down to One:
"Paradise is simple as the simple dew.

Blond Life, raw, unadorned,
Is apple enough when we feel adored.
—Settle quick the pipping kettle, Kate,
And kiss the kittens twice.— Unintended
Heaven whistles wettest, when we forget

Ourselves."

'ROUND MIDNIGHT

Another old poet, old friend, I conjure:
a second Daniel to write to, while I sit
at my pondering pints, pink with drinking—
my ruminative mind returns to me
a hundred hundred hours merrily heaped
with cocksure colloquy, pecking in the shade
of the lion's den, two aging pagans
hailing Pan.   How often we mocked
the very teeth of death with foamy vows
outrageous as their sudsy birth. At midlife,
our fortunes pile up silver dust to fill
our untrimmed temples, a wealth of thoughts
enriched by alpine crowns of time, as if
wreathing clouds consented, trailing
harmless sparks, to be our thinking caps!
Years are mounting as we mount the years:
our sacrifice is *to live,* and remain alienate
from pop culture, embracing what was great.
To linger on Olympus in our skivvies,
our discarded skis set beside the fire;
exchanging grapes with the gods, while midnight
purrs plush, is triumph enough for us.

Sway-stacked and furred with congenial
dust, familiar books look out from under
ragged racks of antique antlers
and bad gags at this seaside pub—
the creak of memory loud underfoot,
a tub of button daisies declaiming spring
beneath the wind-waved sign: Ron's West End.
At this cratered sea-cliff's visionary height,
summer nights, still softly unborn,
and windy winter's diminishing end both
blow round our glowing table talk, whispering
wisdoms between the elbowed
mellow beers and bossy Brunhildas
who rule the roost as if Chaucer never
died, nor no clock ever tolled a verse
beyond Falstaff's everlasting thirst.

We'd talk until our literary prattle
mounted, instance by little instance,
to tallest universals: "Little Man's
imagination floats, lotus-like, seeming
unbound in the water blaze, and yet at its
root, mud and blossom are integral; even thus
is our little man's imagination integral
with Nature's nurturing phenomena—"

Cheerly we keep the "Al-Ron-Quin's"
covenant of converse, alarming charm
of riposte and counterpoint displayed
around the flash and yellow leer of mugs.
Wordsworth's here emending mumbles,
Hamlet hums and haws 'til the deed is done—
both dissed and up-ended by our roaring joy
in favor of old Coleridge and fierce Lear,
one divining lines of logic in the infinite,
one wrangling bare humanity on an empty heath,

barking heartfelt metaphysics with a fool.
And so we argue high midnight through to closing,
and press each other's contention to a peak.

And so a heightened speech is piled,
word on word, and green on green,
in the natural admonition of an oak tower-
ing over lesser growths.   Just as in humid June
we'd climbed far Nether Stowey's stones
in scrambled haste, short-breathed, up
beneath the governing shade of woods
so old and dense all stirring sound was damped
until the hill's bare cap opened in a swirl
of sky—blue and white and misted.
The mountain where we stood, and stand,
(the round high hill where Coleridge crowed
until a last disaster buried him beneath),
pours roundness down its sides, mossy coombs
unmoving as the sweating stones they covered:
green beyond the memory of green, everlasting
as the grass where Coleridge strolled in glee.
How long our conversation that day unrolled,
laughing unmannerly as we hopped the brainy turf
above horizons where the sea sketched white
a limit to the vista, and to the sight—
and all the open dome of heaven was mute,
God's own silence by piety magnified.

What awful power moves unseen within us,
blowing potent gusts through us, until we're left
consigned unprepared to pinnacles unguessed?
As music crests and crests to its crescendo,
so poets' lives rise to one resounding note.

Outside Ron's, the sea scowls pewter, too,
an echo of those lonely Stowey views,

agile as a drunken dutchman's fermented brew.
Here, too, Dan, the decay of light and time
declare a limit to the sight;   here the sea
flashes crested in the softly silver eve,
and our old talk billows hollow with the surf,
hazarding new splashes at night's darkest onset.
Above, the unmoored moon—which calls
heart and head and all to dream—repeats
impermanent feats in the expanding scale
all dreams distort and no knowledge amends.
Our littleness is echoed like a fractal's edge
in the universal pattern—as yet unspoken!
And so the jazz of chatter happens, again
and again: sophisticated, false; brave, benighted—

The dissolute smoke that clouds the moon,
the dull confusion of stop-motion, photo-emulsion skies,
where memory and meme are meeting this eve,
is North-Star sharp by midnight, and we see
how monkeys fed on evolution's bread
row on the auroraed sea below, parting lights
with makeshift paddles, as if the whole Milky Way
could sit reflected in the pond out back!
And indeed it does sit there, when we remember
to look with Galileo's lens, or rheumy
Rousseau's ruminative glance.

FROM EVIL INTERLUDES

A fantasy novella about the life of the great French poet,
Charles Baudelaire

...[Charles Baudelaire, supreme poet, discussing poetry with poet Gerard Nerval]

Without the incantation of a formula, there is no science. Lacking science, how can one have a poetry of mists and amulets, razors and daisies? If a heart should miss a beat, but then return to its effortful circulation, the circumlocution of its everyday existence, that petty farce and sham, we are brought to a new knowing of the heart, an awareness that it exists. To stop hearts, that is my experiment. If they start back up again.... Well, I tried. My own one day will forget itself.

How to see reality but through enchantment? How to create a vision that enchants yourself? This is the only difficulty: to be made to believe by words alone, so that reality may be completely blotted out, as in an opium stupor, or lonely Poe upon his lover's tomb chanting verities, and then to dismiss the fiction that has dismissed the world. Ah! That must be what it is like to be alive for a moment. An ocean of feeling—eviscerated!

Is this sanity? Yes, if properly punctuated.

Attend to life, and then depart it. This is how one cultivates the 'voice from beyond the tomb.' Velvet *weltanschauung!*

"Nerval, how shall we blend all effects, all expressions?"

"I forget."

"Do you really? As a child, I was too new to forget anything; everything was too close, too sudden to forget. I had yet to be touched by that magic wand, *Nostalgia*. One needs a death."

"Now I remember."

"That must be a poem!"

...[Years later, Bonadventure, Baudelaire's best friend, at home, before his garden bonfire]

Ah! Young Francois has put away the plates at last; the burnt bits of bacon, always too crisp or too flaccid, fried eggs solid as Gibraltar, cream cheese, mushroom caps, soup thin as a saint's blood, a wicked spray of asparagus that mocked my inoperant manhood—yes I have advanced to that grim age, Marlene, and even my animal interest has waned along with my wang—some gruyere and jam. A delight, really. And for the topper, a dollop of Nougatine and a sallow slice of dry cake. Hmm.

And now I have returned to my garden, taken up like the taming of Africa by my wife and old Jacques (old even to us!). A new trainline encroaches on our simplicity in the dead distance, sighing to a halt at that satanic gingerbread house concoction of a stop, which I can only think of as the fiendish application of a little girl's nightmarish dreams of a house brought stunningly and wrenchingly to powdered life. Ech! Jacques' one concession to barbarity out here in the garden is due to me—a bonfire pit where I roast my bones in some old man's prelude of Hell, and which I enjoy inordinately even in the swelter of August. I collapse on my old rattan chair, once so new I thought it would never be of service, like the rigid blankness of babies; you never imagine that they could grow into something as useful as a prostitute or an amanuensis. Yet, I have seen both emerge from their swaddling clothes in my passage on earth, and that is another delightful meal for me—of my memory.

Let me see—yes, in this ratty stack of manuscripts, here is all the soiled heart of that genius and compatriot of ours, Baudelaire. Before the bonfire, which is gratefully releasing my knees from the purgatory to which they have been condemned daylong, is the right place to read one last time, such words of fire:

"'Forgive them, Lord, for they know not what they do.'
Too true, too often! Our eyes are clotted with cancerous
growths, we plunge into the abyss not knowing one thing from
the next. Thinking to do good, we execute the innocent;
harping on virtue, we innoculate the guttersnipe against
reforms; blessed by a bounty of spirit or nature, we waste both
and grumble at our spendthrift style! It seems to me that the
only sure delight can come, must come, through the certainty
of sacrilege; to know the good and to knowingly disobey. To
have the mind of Jesus and the perversity of the Devil. For, by
doing so, we at least *know* what we are doing, and are not just
rockets let loose in the mist. In this way, all of our morality
has the utilitarian angle of an angel's mirror: we see ourselves,
not as we would be (as occurs in the instructive mirror of
church) but as we are, by our willful deformity from the
indestructible elegance set before us.

"Woman—take the savage in her natural state: her
lyricism is that of the bestial mass, the 'beast with two backs.'
There is no exaltation of the essential self in such an act;
there is only a total and self-degrading abasement before
another, an acknowledgement of need, an exchange of uses, as
at an agricultural fair. It is the sick bargain between the abject
gambler and the croupier—one agrees to give up all he has;
the other, equally debased, agrees to accept the debt. A
disgusting exchange! Nothing is given, all is hard trading and
walleyed vision. Despicable!

"We sex where we excrete. God has jammed our noses in
the foul joke; the moaning misnomer named 'love.'

"George Sand is one of these women, crying like a
mounted hen about her glorious degradation. 'I have
humiliated the men by taking my pleasure with them! haha!'
That they have turned her pages, or cut into her supple fonts
does not appear to have crossed that great empty gap she calls
her 'mind, invincible and indivisible.' The artist never tears
himself into needs, petty dramas or lazy lapses of the integral
vision; his abysses are interior *only!* He never comes out to

play. He remains maestro and intimate only with himself. The stage of life is a sham which never attains anything of interest; copulation is the entry under another's proscenium—the artist never leaves the green room of himself.

"All love is prostitution of the purer impulse. The more a man sates his sex on the arts, the less randily he hankers after the mottled artifact (of the woman, the man, or the child). If one is to choose degradation as a sensation, an artistic experience and type or route of salvation from dim ennui, only the ideal of degradation will serve the turn. Congress with Satan, fly the church perch of the limited self in the direction of homely Hades; invoke the delights of the damned, and tell yourself that you are going down, down, down—all the way. To seek God carries the insecurity of a lust for promotion in another's incomprehensible eyes; patience, humility, and a divine sign are all required passwords for this tourney of the soul. Uncertainty of the limitless light! I renounce the doubtful path—although it rises to Heaven itself!

"Every kind word is a kiss in the mist, uncertain of where its finally planted; every curse condemns with surety."

I put my old feet closer to the flaring conflagration, causing the glittery cinders to crack and grind.

"To lose one's way in the sewers of the flesh; all the annals of love throughout time are but the jottings of sanitation superintendents.

"Strip down to your virginity, then lave it with gravesores. This is the only likely turnpike."

The paper browns at its edges and sashays in the updraft before turning a double somersault and crumpling to its utter destruction. It is so beautiful to watch the light take away the inky weight of the words, their dirty intrusion onto the page. Now another page flies, fumbles, and folds. It seems that, as an artist, I have turned to burning. The beautiful soul-croaks of my friend—chasing oblivion once again (and, I pray, finally) in the flames.

Here in this garden bonfire, I reverse the heroism of embattled Byron. Instead of pulling the boiling organ from the conflagration, I here consign to fire the scattered pages that Charles had described to me one day in his last illness as *My Heart Laid Bare*.

FROM THE SINGING WELL

A YA novel of magic and growing up

Chapter Eleven, "Further In"

Granny, Sarah, and Barnabas (who seemed more resigned than surprised to hear that magical enemies resided in Traeshurstaene) discussed the possible implications of Granny Pansy's insights. Granny Pansy backed off of her assertion that "enemies" were aware of what Sarah's singing had awakened. Perhaps Sarah had merely roused the old magic inadvertently. And then again, perhaps not. Granny felt they needed to be certain before they could proceed. She hadn't lived in the town herself in several years. She would have to get "the lay of the land," as she said before she could know how to proceed in these magical matters. That's what she had been doing with the cauldron, trying to create a window into current events—a sort of way of going "through the mirror," as she put it. But all she had been able to discern was a fog in the other realm, dim activity taking place in a thickening mist. An occasional figure bobbed closer to the surface now and again, but not with any reliable clarity.

"You're quite strong yourself, child," Granny noted. "Your voice has grown into a surgical dagger, and can cut through in any direction. Such a skill, used without training, might on its own arouse the Gods of Autumn, or hurry along some sequence of events."

"My voice?" inquired Sarah. "You mean just because I was singing their names, the Gods of Autumn are reappearing?"

"Well, it may be child. The old gods are always just under the surface of things, anxious for any chance to break back into the world of active mischief."

"Can that truly be so?" doubted Barnabas. "I didna see naught, as I told ye. And Sarah herself was sort of tranced, as if sleepwalkin'."

"Hmm," mused Granny Pansy. "The gods' careless havoc is just the sort of sowing of confusion that our enemies would delight in."

"Are you sure you're not leap-froggin' yer guesses, Gram Tone?"

"No," she admitted. "I am not sure. I'm not sure at all. What we need is some hard intelligence, and not this frivolous guesswork."

Granny Pansy had put her hat on a chair and was pacing the kitchen nervously, hands clasped behind her back. The sight of her Granny Pansy looking so uncertain was in many ways the scariest thing Sarah had seen yet.

"Well," said Granny Pansy finally. "Why don't you and Abbey go play outside after you've had a shower and cleaned up from your misadventure, young lady. And when you do go outside, wear that pendant on the outside of your blouse. Barnabas, keep an eye on those two, would you please? I have to go into town for a little while and pick up some supplies and whatnot. I'll take Dar with me."

"Granny Pansy, can't I come into town with you? I don't want hang around and play with Abbey."

"Why not, she's your cousin. And you've hardly had any time to get to know each other. Why, when I was a girl, my cousin Charlie and I had all sorts of adventures all over Traeshurstaene. Those are memories that I still value, and lessons that I could've learned in no other way, my dear."

"All right," moped Sarah, who knew better than to argue with her grandmother.

"I'll keep an eye on the pair o' them," promised Burrbuckle.

* * *

"We'll go no farther than the Crossamum Falls," Barnabas Burrbuckle informed Sarah and Abbey as their Grandmother drove away in her son's ramshackle station wagon. "I've promised yer Grammum."

Sarah and Abbey looked about as thrilled as a pair of pooches in the dog pound.

"Barnabas, as long as we're going to be spending the day playing together, would it be all right if I called up Missy and had her come over too?"

"And Shelly too," added Abbey quickly.

"Yes, and Shelly too," agreed Sarah.

"Well, I don't know," thought Barnabas aloud. "Yer Grammum didna say one way or t'other about having more friends come by."

"Well, if she didn't say ..." began Sarah.

"Then its up to you," finished Abbey.

Barnabas looked at the empty driveway where Ganny Pansy had just left.

"It's just a couple of friends," said Sarah persuasively.

* * *

The four girls were chatting away like a brood of birds as they skipped along ahead of the lumbering Barnabas Burrbuckle. Occasionally a ripple of giggles would flit through them as they enjoyed the cold afternoon. They all had good hats and coats on, but Barnabas made sure that Sarah kept her pendant plainly visible on the outside of her clothing.

The afternoon went by before any of them were aware of it, including Barnabas, who enjoyed watching over the girls with a sort of Dutch uncle's indulgence. Before any of them expected, they could hear the gurgling sound of Crossamum Falls just beyond the next turn in the road. It was that very waterfall from which the fabled Aedh was said to have leaped when her true love was slain in battle.

"Look!" noticed Missy Quicknass, running ahead and away from the path toward a low stone wall that ran along the dirt roadway. "An overturned turtle! Let's get him right side up again."

The other girls gathered to Missy's side swiftly. They were examining the markings on the underside of the turtle's shell. It was a very large turtle, at least two and a half feet in diameter. Barnabas looked down with a mild curiosity, making sure that this wasn't a snapping turtle that might mistake a little girl's finger for a tasty worm.

The turtle's slow legs rotated at the four quarters of its shell, churning mildly in the crisp autumn air. "There's where he went awry," noted Barnabas, pointing at a sloped rock in front of the tortoise, leading through what seemed to be a large break in the stone wall. "He fell off of his sunning stone, I've little enough doubt."

The girls knelt down by the opening, trying unsuccessfully to shove the turtle over, while Barnabas got to his knees, and lifting the heavy tortoise easily, set it on its legs in the grass. Once having regained its freedom, the turtle set off sluggishly. Just as the children were about to set off down the path again themselves, out-racing the turtle in a few skipping strides, Barnabas caught sight of something that disturbed him through the crevice in the wall.

"He walks kind of like Mr. Burrbuckle," said Missy, looking at the turtle. The other girls all laughed. They were in high spirits, thrilled to be only under the permissive purview of Barnabas.

"Oh," chuckled Abbey, doing a fair, if squeaky, impression of Burrbuckle. "I wouldna say he's all that slow-footed."

"Hush now," came in Barnabas in a harsh whisper. "There's them that we wouldna want ta hear us just across the way."

The girls immediately fell silent and crowded close to the wall. Five pairs of eyes looked across an empty backyard at an ungainly Victorian house that perched on a sandy hilltop, with one crooked, bare tree beside it. Four long shadows marched down the slope toward Barnabas and the children, crossing to a basement entrance at the side of the house in the gathering dusk. Two black cars had moments before swum into view along the noisy gravel drive. It was the loud sound of the cars' rapid braking that had first alerted Barnabas to the fact that someone was on the other side of the wall. There looked to be three adults and a child. Between two of the larger figures, a long box was being handled. It seemed to be quite heavy, causing the men to walk with deeply bent knees. All of them could hear the basement entrance clang shut with a shudder. After a few more moments, when no one else appeared from the cars, the girls began to pepper Barnabas with questions.

"Who is that?" started Abbey.

"Why must we stay secret from them?" added Shelly, looking bemused by Barnabas Burrbuckle's continuing to stoop lower than the stone wall.

"Are they the enemy?" asked Sarah tensing up visibly in her crouch.

"What enemy are you talking about, Sarah," said Missy, clearly astonished to hear such a word. The other girls turned surprised faces toward Sarah, who continued to look intently at Barnabas, hoping against hope that he would tell her "No." For clearly, these must be the very people they were warned against at the breakfast table. And for all his doubting then, Barnabas had taken every syllable of Granny Pansy's warnings with utter seriousness. When Sarah didn't answer, the girls all turned toward Barnabas too, and looked up into his large, kind but impassive face like so many flowers turned toward the sun.

"Well, now," said Barnabas slowly. "We'd best be on toward home."

The girls waited to see if Barnabas would add anything to this laconic summation. But when he continued silent, and made as if to turn back up the road, the girls all erupted in a sing-song of protest.

"Hush now. Hush now!" Barnabas commanded. But it was too late. None of the girls would stay quiet until they at least got some answers. None, that is, except Sarah, who looked fixedly through the gathering shadows at the narrow house up the slope.

"I may as well tell you what is there, so that you'll all agree to go back quietly," Barnabas began. "A peep's as good as a roar when yer bein' hunted, me Da always said."

Barnabas gave the girls an abbreviated lowdown on what had been happening to Sarah.

"You mean all that's happened to you, and you haven't breathed a word to me!" said Missy, thoroughly offended. "Well, you won't keep me out of your adventures any longer, I'll tell you."

"Adventures?" said Sarah, incredulous at her friend's attitude. "Are you insane? You don't have any idea what those people in there could be doing."

"Well, neither do you," Missy countered reasonably. "And neither do any of us. What do we know about magic?"

The other girls looked at Missy with blank faces.

"What we need to do," she continued, also reasonably, "is investigate."

In moments, all the girls had taken up Missy's cause. All except for Sarah, that is. Sarah stood quietly looking at the house, now black in the spreading twilight. The full moon was on the wane. The only light coming from the house was a twinkling glimmer in a single basement window.

"Well, Sarah," began Barnabas. "You mun say. It's your fate more'n ours what goes on in yonder house. I'll abide by your decision. Toward home, or to the house?"

Sarah didn't turn or make any gesture that acknowledged Mr. Burrbuckle's words. She continued to contemplate the house in the distance. Finally, she said, quite simply, but with a look the seemed as if she was about to vomit, "the house."

"Bravely said, Sarah" approved Missy.

"More'n you are like to know," said Barnabas with a quiet respect. Sarah began to move through the crack in the wall, and Barnabas put his hand out in front of her. "No, that's not to happen. I'll go first, crawlin' and sidewinding up the slope to the winder. When I get there, I'll signal for you lot to come on up after." The girls all nodded in unison. "If I don't get fried by some wizard's lightning bolt, that is," he ended with a grim smile.

"If anything happens, anything at all, even if its just a fox slippin' through the underbrush, you lot just high-tail it back to the main road, and flag down a car to take you all home."

And with that, the ungainly laborer put his cap in the front pocket of his jacket, and slithered through the narrow opening just as gamely as a snake. The girls watched him carefully, and were impressed by the fact that, even though they were watching him the entire time, they still lost track of him in the high grass and shadows no less than three times. They were all surprised when, several long minutes later, they saw his outline waving his cap in the flickering light thrown by the basement window. The girls threw themselves down in the grass and tried their best to imitate the expert infiltration that Barnabas had just demonstrated for them.

The girls lay in a deflated semi-circle around Barnabas, flat on the ground, their legs splayed. They had chosen their spots carefully, and if anyone had looked out from that basement window, the most they would have thought they saw were ten blinking fireflies clinging to the frosted grass.

Inside the basement, Mr. Plimsoul and his lady friend from the Political Committee meeting were bowing with great concentration over the long box that had been carried in earlier. It was set on a pair of sawhorses, and was as slick and black as a coffin. Around the pair, and around the coffin-like box, strode Mr. Hecatomb and a small, very ugly, man. They were holding braziers of incense, which let our thin streams of scented smoke that penetrated even the night air outside where the girls and Barnabas lay watching.

"What is that stuff made of," hissed Missy Quicknass, unable to stop herself from commenting. "It smells like burnt rattlesnakes."

Just at that moment, the woman in the basement straightened up. She looked around with a whiplike speed. She seemed to ask a question imperiously of all within the basement. Her boa, the same she'd had on the other week, writhed with a sinewy agitation as if alive.

Everyone on the lawn held their breaths. It would not do to have such a woman notice your existence.

Mr. Plimsoul turned his head, and seemed to say a few sharp words over his shoulder. The woman looked subtly annoyed by his insolence, but after a considered moment, snapped her own command at the dwarf and then turned back to face the box with Plimsoul.

The dwarf put down his brazier laboriously on the floor of the basement, and then stepped nimbly over to a corner neither the girls nor Barnabas had a view of, and then returned with a peeling ladder which he put up against the wall with a startling clack. In a moment, they could all see his hideous face pressed up against the basement window. After a short struggle with the latch, the window opened inward; a brown cloud of smoke huffed from the low window. Missy coughed involuntarily, suppressing it as much as she was able.

"*Gar,*" grumbled the dwarf. "It's a night to catch leeches in."

None of those lying in the grass knew why such a night was a good one to catch leeches in, but apparently, the dwarf would rather have the room full of the hideous smoke they were generating in the ornate braziers than the clean night air. Now, at least, the children and Barnabas could hear the conversation happening in the basement with relative ease.

Lois Marie Harrod

LIKE A MAELSTROM WITH A NOTCH

Emily Dickinson

And when the clothing factory collapsed
in Dhaka, Bangladesh, one young seamstress
was trapped in the Muslim prayer room
which also stored boxes of skirts and shawls,
shirts, sheers, socks and sequins,
and for those in need, a few prayer cloths
thrown over pipes and stretching to a strut or two.

And when that nineteen-year-old was rescued,
it was a miracle because we wanted to believe
that we too can survive, ignorant and inventive,
disregarding the adjacent, the close-by distant
dead, sucking air through shaky pipes, licking
the leaking rain, yes, washing our faces, knowing
whatever those gods of mercy had done to others
they had not yet done it to us. That miracle.

And of course, to keep sane, she did find things to do,
packed and unpacked the boxes of saris in her little room,
maybe the first she had ever had to herself,
changed her clothes repeatedly as teenagers do,
why not, hadn't she always wanted to try them on?–
so that after seventeen days when someone at last
heard her cry, she was wearing a radiant red scarf
around her neck, as if she had just tripped off a runway–
a scarf any one of us might buy for almost nothing.

Penny Harter

DARNING SOCKS

The hole usually wears in the heel
after the wool has thinned, so that
held against the morning, one sees
a patchwork, a woven crossing
of strands. And then the hole,

appears, calling for needle and yarn,
for stitches to be made around the
circle or tear, then criss-crossed back
and forth to weave endurance, to patch
what can be for a little longer.

Wounds after surgery are often closed
with staples, or glued against chance
opening. Inner wounds are stitched
by skilled surgeons whose hands
have practiced darning flesh.

Whether socks or mortal meat be
mended, held up to either sun or moon
the sky will break through, haloing
the edges of all wounds, then sealing
them with light.

John Hoppenthaler

DOLPHINS AT POINT PLEASANT BEACH

A sudden pod gathers a throng together
to gawk by the water. It's rare, their half-
mooning close along the break line.

Wearing official red trunks, lifeguards
keep us from slipping in, from lingering
a few moments just beyond the reach of curious

sunbathers, envious creatures so merely
tethered to beach sand. And now one leaps
free of surf, flashes a second, silver,

rockets through space. But soon
it splashes down, and then dolphins
emerge in their expected place,

removed enough to seem unreal, dreams
tilted toward horizon. Jutting fins
cut the tin-gray surface, summon

the stray shadow of what goes on in there,
what's partial and nearly human,
a mystery we watch swirl, then disappear.

Theresa Irwin

Theresa Irwin is a professional opera singer who enjoys writing and recording impressions of the world around her. As a youngster, she was urged to join her high school creative writing class where her first published work appeared in the school magazine.

Later, her singing career launched her into unexpected positions where publicity was an important factor and writing press releases became a necessity. Soon, she was designing press releases, pamphlets and fliers for the Monmouth Civic Chorus and the Night on Broadway Company. As editor of the monthly newsletter for the MCC, she interviewed several members each month and wrote lively profiles for each individual.

In 2002, a story submitted to the Asbury Park Press was printed *in statu quo.* Wanting to improve her writing skills, in 2008 she completed a correspondence course of Writing for Children and Teenagers with the Institute of Children's Literature.

Upon her aunt's death in 2010, she inherited a folder of her aunt's published poetry; a discovery which led her to the Jersey Shore Poets, where she explores her own hidden ability for writing poetry.

Presently, she is in the process of revising and editing her memoirs.

MOTLEY OF BOOKS

A maze of books
  in musty rows.
A quaint old shop
  of timeless prose.
I drift through aisles,
  where silent voices
  trapped in print—
hold myriad choices.

Books are like friends,
  treasures to behold.
Have few, but well chosen;
  rare as fine gold.

A FADED ROSE

Yesterday, I found a rose
growing in my garden.
I clipped the beauty
with blushing hue,
displayed it in my parlor.
When came the dawn,
I found it faded;
petals sagging sadly.

No more the beauty when first I held
that prize within my hand. I rudely
plucked it from the vase,
and tossed it in good haste.

Today, I am that rose
growing in a garden. A life

of splendor have I seen.
Yet, stealthily comes tomorrow's dawn.
in silent steady streams.

Oh, MY BROTHER

Our four room apartment was in a five story tenement.
Noise was all around and people galore.
Despite the crowds, I was filled with contentment,
   though we lived in the back on the second floor.

I followed my brother. He led the way.
Whatever he asked, I was quick to obey.
He asked in a whisper, "Have ya any money?"
He was my hero and so very funny.

He had a good ear and whistled on pitch.
A homemade xylophone, he said, was a cinch.
He lined up mom's glassware with water alone,
   and measured the amount in each glass for tone.

We trapped mice in the kitchen on many a night,
Made the poor little critters scurry with fright.
The games he made up were too many to tell.
Life in the city was no farmer's dell.

I recall the events of how it was then.
He was eighteen years old, and I was just ten.
He bought a thirty-two Pontiac, his very first car
Which overnight quickly made him a star.

The boys on the street flocked to his side,
   tongues hanging out. They wanted to ride.
He revved up the motor. He told them, "Hop in!"

We were off to the Bronx for a bite and a spin.
We ate at White Castle. It was a surprise
   to eat tiny hamburgers like quarters in size.

My brother was drafted when age twenty-one,
   a painful "Goodbye" to my mother's son.
Destiny steered him to the Korean War.
As his ship sailed off to that far distant shore,
Mama's eyes filled up with abundant tears.
As for Papa, in all my years,
He never cried—
Except that day when part of him died.

Wounded in battle of the "Iron Triangle,"
My brother asked questions too hard to untangle.
So when his heart began to groan,
He clearly made the fight his own—the fight for him to get
   back home.

MUSES OF A YOUNG GIRL

The blossom of your smile
 growing from the warmth of your heart
  brings Spring to my soul.

The twinkle in your eye
   is the brightest of stars
   shining in the sky.

               * * *

At first it was a spark
 hidden and out of sight.

And then a blazing fire
burning in the night.

* * *

A summer field,
a distant song,
a lonely pasture,
where I belong.

A ROOFTOP

Way up there, high above the city streets,
Where traffic noise is muffled,
And children's playful shrieks,
Blend strangely all together
    in a murmur soft and sweet.

A forest of antennae engulf me as I stare
    at a multitude of pigeons,
    calmly circling through the air.
A line of clothes hung out to dry,
    allows the wind a playful spree.
My spirit soars to the open sky,
    up on a rooftop where I am free.

Charles H. Johnson

SIXTY-FOUR

(To Lainey)

*"This thought is death, which cannot choose
But weep to have that which it fears to lose."*
                    William Shakespeare

Snow descends gently outside my window
Silently growing higher on the ground
Until no trace remains of where to go,
No guiding path to walk can be found.
Relentlessly white washes color away;
It clings to bare brown limbs starting to bend
Beneath the building weight painting the day.
This canvas pleases like a newfound friend.
So too my thoughts of you when they appear
And fall silently to blanket my mind
With joy and beauty I want to be near –
These my whole life's travels I sought to find.
Like snow you delight me with something new
Whenever your quiet magic's on view

Victoria Kaloss

Victoria Kaloss is a writer and poet. She has been published in The Atlantic Highlands Herald, Poetic Reflections of Monmouth County, Monmouth County Magazine, poetsonline.org, Insights, Wicked Banshee Press, Howl of Sorrow: A Collection of Poetry Inspired by Hurricane Sandy and Long Dumb Voices.

She earned three points in a Spoken Word LoserSlam battle— one of her most extreme accomplishments.

She is an active member of IWWG.

Victoria has lived with rheumatoid arthritis since infancy. She has overcome multiple joint replacement surgeries and considers herself to be distantly related to The Bionic Woman.

Victoria chronicles life with a disability and a learned attitude of belief on her website: LivingLifetotheBestofYourPossibility.com

She is continuously inspired by words.

The healing power of Nature.

The healing power of Dreamtime.

The healing power of a Mustang GT 5.0 Liter convertible.

AFTER THE BLIZZARD

Drop by drop
the icicle outside my window
reminds me

> L
> e
> t
>
> g
> o
>
> L
> e
> t
>
> g
> o
>
> L
> e
> t
>
> g
> o

The icicle melts. Alters.
Reborn as a daffodil

DELICACY

Paper flowers twice the size of our eight year old heads,
folded rainbow tissue paper, folded again and again;
fitted with perfect green plastic wire, entwined in lime pipe
cleaners. Perhaps this is modern public school Maypole,
promise of sun, promise of plenty, promise of rebirth.

Three of us students from art class chosen to be photographed
for the local paper and I had been one of the chosen flower-
makers. We three waited inside during recess as the
photojournalist, the journalist, the teacher in charge, Mrs.
Drum and Miss Fisher, the art teacher, spoke and planned as
we waited silently. But we were eight and restlessness led to
chatter. The photographer, suited and sweating, grays comb-
over wet slicked aside, positioned us on the classroom floor as
the grown-ups finished their adult talking. We knelt on the
linoleum floor. My rheumatoid knees hurt, pain-sharp, cold,
and hard. The photographer asked me to shuffle into another
position. I gritted my teeth, moved in concert with pain.

All adult attention switched to us three, holding our huge
colorful delicate, delicate flowers.
"Move, down further. You're too tall, squat further."
"This is as far as I can go," I replied.
"No, squat, put your behind closer to your heels."
"This is as far…"
Mrs. Drum gently touched his shoulder, whispered into his ear,
explaining my medical condition. He nodded, cleared his
throat and took several photo shots. Bulb residue shined
constant in my eyeballs, in my brain.

That night, I prayed to God. 'Please, God, make me like Penny
from Speed Racer. She's pretty, she runs, she's skinny, she
likes animals and she can move fast, jump and run and kneel.'

Morning sun greeted my waking eyes, my heart filled with
joyful anticipation awaiting my rebirth reflection. I hobbled to
the mirror—just me. Same old me.

The newspaper delivered, my parents seen and read the
published article. The grayscale photograph seemed to demean
the flowers.
"Why aren't you smiling?" they asked.
My colorful self demeaned like a delicate flower until I glanced
out the bay window—forsythia reached out her yellow embrace
promising Mother Nature's colorful bounty and boundless love.

SWEET MEMORIES

When rain
quenches dirt
and the sweetness emerges

I remember you
sweetly kissing my cheek
under the umbrella

and years later, me
kissing your bittersweet coffin
under the funeral tent

CLETUS

Cletus, the Cherokee shaman, packed herbs into his seven
holed sacred pipe, found a sacred Bic.

*'How did you think Hiawatha managed to travel the continents
to create peace back then?' I asked.*

Cletus, a twinkle in his blue eyes drew a puff from his sacred
pipe, turned the seven holed bowl, symbol of our Mother, one
click, 'horseback.'

Smoke stuttered through his stifled laugh, 'horsepower, old
fashioned horsepower.
Spirit, the Great Mystery created life in each and every living
thing, galaxies, created Hiawatha
to be a Peacemaker. Great Spirit carried, seeded our warring
tribes into Peace.
The US Constitution is based largely on the Six Nations Confederacy.'

Cletus nodded, inviting my own prayer be drawn from his pipe.
Accepting, I pulled a soulful drag, watched holy smoke rise
from pipe and my lips—lifting to Spirit, lifting my spirit.

*'Sir, how would Peace become permanent? What can be done
today, for our world?'*

Cletus sucked his pipe stem, symbol of our Father, his eyes
glazed over, cloudy like a molting snake, 'the same way.'

EXTRAS NEEDED

The movie man points.
We follow him down First Avenue
like giddy school children
escorted to special assembly.

Mezzaluna restaurant
transformed into a movie set.
Hardwood floors carpeted in wire.
Skilled workers move in shadows
behind cityscape of equipment;
the actors, a man and a woman, sit
in the center of the dining room,
now a stage.

Extras placed at tables set
with coagulated pasta, drowning salad,
cranberry juice pretends to be wine.
First Director directs, *Talk as if you've known*
each other a lifetime but speak quietly.

We four strangers, a real-estate broker,
a high school student, an actress playing hooky
from her day job and a disabled poet,
practice quiet casual conversation.

What's the movie about? Does anyone know?
One of the characters, I don't know which one,
is out on a first date after losing their spouse on 9/11.
I was in school on 9/11. Where were you?

Art under construction, two hours go by.
Actors sit patiently, staff continuously
measures noses to lenses, crew hammers

circular track, reset cables snap,
tempered shouts and tired laughter.

Director, arms crossed over chest, yells *Action!*
The movie set transforms into a first date
with backdrop of reverent whispers.

HURRY UP AND SLOW DOWN

He's waiting for me.
One hand in pocket
jingling his keys,
free hand pinches bridge
between his clamped eyes,

and the only part
of my disabled
body, capable,
of moving faster

beats

until I stand
until I breathe
like a redwood tree

JUST WALKING

Thompson Middle School has a track behind the building
standing atop a modest man-made hill, surrounded by a small
wooded area.

When school is void of outdoor activities,
Middletown adults gravitate to the soft, crunchy oval;
letting off steam by running, jogging, power walking
or in my case - just walking.

One summer afternoon, as my exercise partner
ran circles around me, a second exhausted commuter
searching for runners high entered the circle; then another
and another, yet another still.

Feeling boxed in, I deviated from the normal path,
beautiful as it was with roosting crows, shady oaks,
patches of endangered jewel-weed
which meant poison ivy's nearby.

I strolled down the incline to Thompson's open field
where pre-adolescents play football, field hockey,
moan through gym class; where grown-up counterparts
practice short-game golf shots.

Keeping close to the brush line, I discovered a mature mullein plant
a majestic four foot silver green leafed cone with gold flowering
crown.

A few steps past the giant healing herb I happened upon a groundhog
at eye level, spread across branches as if lounging upon a hammock.

Fearing he was dead, injured, rabid, I gazed intently on the critter
watching to find his rhythm of breath. I spoke aloud, as nervous
talkers generally do, "Are you alright?"

The creature slowly opened his eyes halfway
and glared at me. He glared at me

like my father did when I disturbed him
as he lied on the couch Sunday afternoons watching golf.
My animal instincts told me then, and now,
just walk away.

MAPLE TREE

Red 'X' painted on
Maple round the corner

a singled out
sun worshipper;
future bundle for
fiery stakes

Her aging trunk
plays on gray;
wisdom color

Flecks of bark
near base
collect like dandruff

Still branches permeate
s p a c e

a canopy of arms,
goddess of compassion

Marked by time

or greatness.

ODYSSEY

Revving Odyssey zooms,
bold Andretti maneuver
between blue painted lines.

Chic driver pirouettes from seat
to public street, exclusive ground—
kept her motor running, lock horn blasting.

My handicapped sticker metronome lagged
I unleashed seatbelt, goaded door with feet,
pivoting from mats to macadam.

Clutched my baker's dozen mail pile, tight,
damp slip from lobbyist to politician's grip.
My monthly check fails any rate of exchange.

My slice reduced from sliver to crumb.
Disabled shrink on demand, condemned mice
behind walls, barely heard, rarely seen.

My labored steps ramp negative internal dialogue
sanctioning my low status entrance.
Odyssey driver boogies back to special place.

High heels snap, a two-timing ship-shape dancer.
She's in a hurry. Snubs behind-the-timers, transfixed
narcissist ignores mourning dove nest in oak's wrinkled curve;

jets by the letter carrier on the bench, on break,
juts his face into sunlight, smiles a broad smile,
sighs a contented sigh.

The illegal entitled diva, a cheered victorious priority,
missed the epic happy ending noted
by mystical cripple with nothing but time.

RAIN CLOUDS

Sitting in the vinyl chair,
kitchen window half open,
autumn eagerly nips my bare shoulder;
time for tank tops is over.

Grey clouds stretch across the sky
dewy dust balls collecting
reclaimed multi-facet tears
from rounded corners of the world.

Rain begins to fall.
As Jersey soil is nourished,
faint scents of mint and mold
push through the screen.

Drops fall hard
like a boy crying for his lost dog.
Hard, as a widow weeps
over a single hole.

Collective mist
rolls down red dogwood leaf,
joyful tears of a waltzing bride
and a boy finding his dog.

RATS ARE IN MY BLOOD

My Grandpa Jones, a coal miner,
relied on fellow underworld dwellers.
Furry alarms for invisible gases,
unfelt vibrations.

Rats served Grandpa.

Other crew became annoyed
when bloody vermin
helped themselves to wifely
duty packed lunches.

Grandpa did not share sides
with his hard-hat buddies.
Instead, he packed
extra morsels in his pail,
leaving crumbs, here and there,
along his black belly route.

Rats were family to Grandpa.

WINDOWS

As a small child I wanted the window—craved light, craved a hint
of outside; cotton candy clouds, black crows, peek-a-boo tree branches.
I may have been driven mad—if not for the window.
Perhaps my crib, a bar lined cell—perhaps a past-life
memory in mad house,
certifiable for present life DNA prison—if not for the window.

My mother spun tales, odd sounds from my nursery-
day, night, all the in-between times
Scrape, scrape, scrape—
Drove her mad, worry at first, until she witnessed me pushing,
swaying inside my white second hand crib, across worn oak floors;
distressed planks from crib leg divots leading to the window.

The window my greatest want, the window in my nursery, the window
in my bedroom, the window seat on the bus, the window in my
hospital rooms, the window in my home office, the window in my
poet's soul, always, the window, the window, the window

always—the window's
shapeshifting light

THROUGH ARTHRITIC EYES

I am amazed by
the simplest motions,

the way the bank teller's finger
bends like a hook
as she strikes the keys,

the way a swimmer hoists
his body out of the pool, wrists bent,
hands flat on wet concrete,

the way Sue, my neighbor kneels
planting tulip bulbs,
dirt on bony knees,

the way my nephew flies
down hardwood stairs,
toes gripping edges,

the way my sister files toenails
leaning forward,
chin over bended knee,

the way the young girl sits
Indian style on grass,
watching the caterpillar crawl,

the way the toddler jumps
in the cereal aisle
pointing at red boxes,

the way his mother effortlessly
lifts him onto her hip,
reaching Captain Crunch together,

the way I smile
at the grandness of
the simplest motions.

SANDY'S BEEN HERE

Sandy's been here; No bronze plaques mark her arrival
Along local roads, her marks marred
Deep within heartlands, wetlands, her marks erratic and
unexpected like excised black beauty marks
Her scars mimic raised bumps in the road,
undergrowth uprooted, their bases tilted exposing dirt,
stringy vined roots; a dismembered motherboard—electrical mess.
She came and she went, steel instruments sliced metered tissue,
earth blood sprayed, puddled, pooled across the landscape.
Obstinate wind scraped topsoil, bent cattails, flattened Indian grass,
trees splintered into toothpicks—deadwood dangles, publically, hung to rot.
Her images scattered across the lands, she mopped the beachfront
redistributing sand where it is meant to be—
She redistributed the land and the masses,
Seaside Heights Ferris wheel, blown, thrown, held under saltwater
suffocated, drowned, corroding
divided Sea Bright
separated deviated bridges, left barrier islands in her wake,
changed appearance reversed face lift, turned tar into sand,
beaches into landfills, flipped homes into boathouses,
indoor pools, danger zones—no lifeguard on duty.
Sandy's watery Hell baited nightmares, surprise gigantic water wall—
a collective catastrophe manifesting fast heartbeats, saltwater sweat,
fire under layered skin.
The people lost sleep, lost homes, lost money, memories,
peace of mind, the politicians gained steam ahead publicity,
peace of mind Stronger than the Storm money deals, rebuilt
commerce kick-backs, demolition kicks-down civilians, drop
kicked into a black and blue sea

Drop dead beauty is skin deep, beauty marks
demand deep inspection—search and rescue,
look deep, under topsoil, ponder over actions

before pushing up without daisies.
Can't escape ramifications for altering the land,
dumping poisons in water, taxing air, look, right up there,
and there, there—look deep, under there, and there, there.
Sandy's been here; her beauty marks permanent
revolting tattoo.

X. J. Kennedy

THOMAS HARDY'S OBSEQUIES

As related by a guide at Max Gate, Dorsetshire

When Hardy perished, torn between
A Dorset graveyard and the Abbey,
Folks whispered a peculiar tale
Whose central figure was a tabby.

It was decreed that Hardy burn
And satisfy each bookish mourner
By being honored with an urn
Of ashes in the Poets' Corner,

But he had chosen other ground,
His native earth, in which to rest,
And so a compromise was found:
A surgeon probed the great man's breast,

Dispatched inside a biscuit tin
His excised heart out to the yard
Of Stinsford Church for placement in
Ground that his forebears' gravestones guard.

But soon the sexton coming for
The poet's disembodied pumper
Found the tin empty on the floor,
The house cat grinning, belly plumper.

Well, what to do? Despairing not,
They sheared the cat of all nine lives,
Interred her in a flowered plot
Flanked by the first and second wives,

A fate that Hardy might have planned,
Ironic—he'd have relished that—
    A wife on either handless hand,
    A heart whose casket is a cat.

Adele Kenny

WITHOUT SEEING

It isn't now or this patch of blue autumn, light skimmed like milk without substance (its ghost on my lips). Or the way trees darken before the sky, the way light slants through pines (my neighbor's lamp or the moon). It's not the way night feels when I walk in March, when snow melts into mud, and I smell grass again; when I know, without seeing, that tight buds open high in the branches. It's not the expected order of things but moments of *other* (when something startles you into knowing *something* other).

Tonight, wind pulled leaves from the sky to my feet and, suddenly (without warning) a deer leapt from the thicket behind me—leapt and disappeared—past me as I passed myself, my body filled with absence, with air, a perfect mold of the light gone through it.

Ted Kooser

AFTER YEARS

Today, from a distance, I saw you
walking away, and without a sound
the glittering face of a glacier
slid into the sea. An ancient oak
fell in the Cumberlands, holding only
a handful of leaves, and an old woman
scattering corn to her chickens looked up
for an instant. At the other side
of the galaxy, a star thirty-five times
the size of our own sun exploded
and vanished, leaving a small green spot
on the astronomer's retina
as he stood on the great open dome
of my heart with no one to tell.

Jerome Leary

Jerome Leary is a New Jersey State licensed Marriage & Family Therapist in private practice. He is married to Joan. The couple now live in Lincroft, NJ. Jerry is a former Roman Catholic priest. His wife, Joan, is a Spiritual Director and has spent many years as a Pastoral Assistant.

Much of of the inspiration for Jerry's poetry arises from married life and from his own spiritual quest which began in his childhood, growing up in an Irish Catholic home where night prayers and the Rosary were a daily practice. Literature, including poetry, were also a normal part of every day life.

Jerry is a graduate of Mount Saint Mary's University and Seminary, Emmitsburg, Maryland. He holds a graduate degree in Pastoral Counseling from Iona College, New Rochelle, New York. After leaving the priesthood Jerry continued his work as a Counselor.

Jerry's initiation into the world of poetry was a family affair. He writes about growing up with a father and uncle who read their poems which were specially composed for family gatherings. Eventually, they would read some of Jerry's first efforts. Such an honor! And he would continue to write throughout high school, college and seminary. Jerry's poetry would often appear in his school's periodicals.

Jerry has been a member of New Jersey poetry groups for over thirty years—most recently, as a member of the *Jersey Shore Poets.* His poems have appeared in various group anthologies: *Voices Rising From the Grove; Poetic Reflections of Monmouth County; Spindrift; Monastic Muse.* He has been published in *Exit 13; Review for Religious,* and in a commemorative Red Bank Library publication.

(Readers can see how Jerry works to stretch an epigrammatic style, using the occasional Villanelle, Pantoum, Sestina.)

SEASCAPE

Fresh colors
snap out
above the day;
busy tides dress, undress
modestly.

We walk
to see
where spiders
hang filigree
amid jetty rock
against the sea.

THE HOARDER

He keeps vague fears of pain within his rooms:
Collects, collects false hope of final gain.
A life when so protected never blooms.

"Abandonment and loneliness I'll store as wounds."
Again, again he plays this dark refrain.
He keeps vague fears of pain within his rooms,

As every stack on stack in danger looms,
Narrows down each walking lane.
A life, when so protected, never blooms.

The stench of inside storage sours to fumes,
While scent of outside worlds drive him insane.
He keeps vague fears of pain within his rooms.

The sound, for him, of neighbor's knock still looms.
From interest in old friends he must abstain!
A life, when so protected, never blooms.

The value of mere storage never grooms;
Corrupts a home into mere place, a final bane.
He keeps vague fears of pain within his rooms.
A life when so protected never blooms.

PUTTING OUT THE TREE

Oh Tannenbaum, still lovely as I leave you,
breathing from uprooted life
with final scent, too sweet, too generous,
incensing me with your forgiveness—
I've sung about you many times,
but never felt so sad.

RIVER LIBRARY

Red Bank's book-spirit
Feeds on this quiet space
Of shore, harboring
Three quarters of a century;
Flows toward a hundred years
As rivers flow
Unendingly.

PRAYER TO ABRAHAM

Naked, when
first called out
beneath erotic stars,
left standing there:
young desire,
uncircumcised by christian saints,
I called through years,
still call,
and no one comes
to clothe my ignorance.

"Abraham, with doubt
still in my loins,
I pray my seed
fill firmaments as grace
released: one final urge toward self,
obedient to love; and,
when emptied out,
join you in light."

PARANOID

Suspicious engines drove him on:
Read a threat in each event;
Smiles he saw as churlish smirks,
No part of life is left benign.

Read a threat in each event;
Chance letters grouped as anagrams.
No part of life is left benign.
A neighbor's nod becomes a sign.

Chance letters grouped as anagrams;
Each license plate, each strange device;
A neighbor's nod became a sign;
Tap-tap-tapping through the night;

Each license plate, each strange device;
The girl downstairs taps taps the pipes;
A neighbor's nod becomes a sign;
Sounds off-and-on, thoughts duplicate;

The girl downstairs taps taps the pipes
Invites nocturnal rendezvous,
Sounds off-and-on, thoughts duplicate
Ways they must communicate;

Invites nocturnal rendezvous
Yet, never chance a face-to-face.
Ways they must communicate;
Through walls and floors and tapping pipes.

Yet, never chance a face-to-face.
Imagined smiles as churlish smirks
Through walls and floors and tapping pipes,
Suspicious engines drove him on.

OCEAN GROVE: A PSALM

Let each generation rest comfortably
Tenting here.
Distant ships
Explore fresh hope,
As with each pull of tide,
Feels grace
In what is new and old—
For within this sacred place,
Again, again,
Sabbath swells
In sounds of thanks.

LE JARDIN A VETHEUIL: MONET (1840-1926)

Watercolor's muted play
reach tall and soft.
Mother and dream-children wake in tunneled light;
step on puddled blue;
feel shadowed warmth of sunflower days.
One child seems to wait.

Dream-child cannot wait;
moves down paths to play
in wakeful colored days:
gold blossoms soft
mix gray with blue
beneath dim morning light.

How mothers pause in changing light
as shadow-wagons wait;
bring children dreams. On gray-blue
here still at play

between tall-flower's soft,
soft innocence of days.

How mothers' thoughts can wound these days,
as sunflowers turn from light;
they hope each child might wait
a bit before they start real play:
gold hardens quick to blue,
where once it had been soft,

now puffs beneath cold blue,
weighs down; blends flower-days;
paints dreams. Yet, children, still at play,
still trust in fading light—
for mothers know where shadows wait,
plead paints dry, colored soft.

Late summer, still soft,
weaves tight this gray with blue.
Children don't know why mothers wait
upon half-spent summer days,
still pause in a paths of light.
Near early Autumn play—

dream-moods of coming days:
how gray-blue dreams of light;
how light-dreams wake to play.

SHADOW LAKE

Autumn waits for her by shadowed lake.
She joins its faded trees;
Steps out into a windlessness.
Sweeps off a patio they seldom used—
Hears Parkway sounds
Through tired light.

MY DANCE

Naked, I danced grotesquely, once,
outlandishly before my wife,
dressed only in a stereo:
loud, up and down, just up and down,
again, again: the drunken props I made of steps:
ascend, descend to twirl and whirl,
twist on and on. . . yet, why?
Why never so inspired, again
to craft staid life in light ballet;
present myself before my Love;
express beyond such words as these,
gift of everything I must profess—
expressed, full-bodied, once,
and unashamed?

BLOOMFIELD AVENUE

I trolley, once again, on iron wheels:
West Essex, Newark and back,
along its strip of cobblestone,
urban to suburban ride,
a retrospect of innocence
of what would finally come,
corner stop to corner stop:
faces of slow change
unrecognized. For me,

such little sufferings then—
get on, get off, get on, get off;
I lean into the Montclair hill;
gain horsepower for the climb

up to Verona heights. Its factory of flags
wave power as awful hidden change,
accelerates to what seems speed
of years down Caldwell flats
that parallel Dad's **Erie** line
across from Grover Cleveland's place,
still undisturbed, mere history;
just mustached face for me:
a nation still asleep.

Last stop, the turnabout,
when turnabouts meant "end"—
But, when I felt a sudden nudge:
"wake up; all tracks are gone!"
My stubborn disillusioned child stayed on:
"I will not recognize your way!"
My dreams keep things the same.

DUET

Side by side, she ripped through William Tell with him;
"Hi Ho Silver, Away!" Left hand, across, flipped pages;
never missed a note (some pages tore, I see), then
accompanied his sea chanteys:
"Many brave hearts are asleep in the deep,
so beware, beware!" The night he died:
arpeggios all night. All night heard four hands,
as two hands searched for life.

DEATH OF A TREE

Men mark off a tree
mechanically;
place orange cones;
make space for this safe work:
first, top-cut each higher branch,
limbs fall in an obedience.

One life's my business, now:
life of one tree—
I will not look away,
where elsewhere, death stays distant
Here, I'm given to brief witness;
mourn as chipper's scream.

A PSALM

Where are you Lord within this darkness!
I feel things moving; sense faint rhythms.
Yet, if on the back of continents each life is carried
And in the charted oceans all things teem,
Why still the soundings of my prayer:
"Unknown! Unknown!"

GUEST ROOM

It's now a mix of years:
wicker chairs now painted red,
rest beneath blue moods of Wedgewood;
place-settings hang with silhouettes of lives
just guessed about,
reduced in size and silence
to one room.

BEFORE THE PARKWAY

All along the route
their patience waned
as roads turned sandier
down to the Jersey Shore

when back ways could not avoid
the open bridge
as one slow thin mast
would paralyze the day
and our front-seating it
pushing crowding forward
"not yet there"
then racing
who'd see the ocean first
rushing towards its vastness
our young lives stretched out
in unending summer
and in one shell
its mystery

FIRST SNOWFALL

First snow quiets me.
Forgives the earth.
Its cold reveals the warmth of linen hills;
lights Birchwood candelabra
placed for short-day feasting.

Diane Lockward

INVECTIVE AGAINST THE BUMBLEBEE

Escapee from a tight cell, yellow-streaked,
sex-deprived sycophant to a queen,
you have dug divots in my yard
and like a squatter trespassed in my garage.

I despise you for you have swooped down
on my baby boy, harmless on a blanket of lawn,
his belly plumping through his orange stretch suit,
yellow hat over the fuzz of his head.
Though you mistook him for a sunflower,
I do not exonerate you,
for he weeps in my arms, trembles, and drools,
finger swollen like a breakfast sausage.
Now my son knows pain.
Now he fears the grass.

Fat-assed insect! Perverse pedagogue!
Henceforth, may flowers refuse to open for you.
May cats chase you in the garden.
I want you shellacked by rain, pecked by shrikes,
mauled by skunks, paralyzed by early frost.
May farmers douse your wings with pesticide.
May you never again taste the nectar
of purple clover or honeysuckle.
May you pass by an oak tree just in time
to be pissed on by a dog.

And tomorrow may you rest on my table
as I peruse the paper. May you shake
beneath the scarred face of a serial killer.
May you be crushed by the morning news.

Susan Martin

Susan Martin, author and poet, retired from teaching English and creative writing after a thirty-two career. She earned her BA degree in English at Cedar Crest College and did graduate work in English at Lehigh University. She also did post graduate work in creative writing and editing at New York University.

As a teacher, she established a proactive creative writing program for her school. Her students competed and often won prizes in local and state competitions. They also submitted their work for publication in outside venues. Several of them became published poets before they graduated from high school. The highlight of their school year was Publication Day, the day when their poetry book to which they contributed and they edited was distributed and celebrated.

She herself has had poetry and short fiction published in several literary magazines, on-line sites, and anthologies. Most recently she has had a short story published in Brandt Street Press' anthology, *Dammit I Love You.* She also had a poem published in *The Lyric,* Spring, 2016, and *The Road Not Taken,* Fall, 2015.

She was a prize winner in Oneal Walters *2009 Women's Inspirational Contest* and the *New Jersey Poetry Society's 2012 Annual Contest.* She got honorable mention in *Torrid*

Literature Journal's Annual Contest, 2014. She is a charter
member of Jersey Shore Poets.

Susan is an avid reader and an inveterate beach bum. Her
idea of the perfect summer day is reading a good book while at
the beach after a swim in the ocean. Many of her poems are
about the Jersey shore.

ACCOUNTS RECEIVABLE

In the corner of my living room
hangs a large abstract painting,
distinct, irregular patterns in primary colors.
If a dermatologist looked at it,
he would say, *Melanoma, big time.*
A cartographer would say, *Ah yes,*
there's Scandinavia, and there's
Italy, kicking Sicily around.
When my husband finished it,
he decided to put it in a show.
It needed a name. That was my job.
At a loss I asked him, *What do you*
think would be an appropriate name?
Off in another world, he asked,
Do you know what we have in
accounts receivable?
That's it, I replied.
We'll call it Accounts Receivable.
Accounts Receivable was sent to the framer.
He called a few days later and said,
We have the frame. Now we need
to put on the wire,
but we don't know which end is up.

A metaphor of life:
You get out of it what you put into it,
it's all about what's due and what's owed,
and does anybody really know
which end is up?

AFTER THE FUNERAL

The house is:
    Clean as a place where no one lives,
    Clean as a conscience the dead forgives,
    Clean as a heart without emotion,
    Empty as love without devotion.

The house is:
    Ordered as nuns as they kneel to pray,
    Ordered as barracks' inspection day,
    Ordered as geese that fly in formation,
    Chaotic as souls that face damnation.

The house is:
    Quiet as an infant sleeping
    Quiet as a widow weeping,
    Quiet as a vacant room,
    The howling of a sated tomb.

AND YOU THOUGHT YOU HEARD IT ALL

So the poor kid suffered from affluenza,
too rich to know the difference
between right and wrong.

I can identify with that.
I have enjoyed poor fiscal health all my life.
Oh, how I suffered from
the maddening itch of credit card crud.
I swiped and I swiped,
but the more I swiped, the worse it got.
It lowered my resistance
until I succumbed to the dreaded
living paycheck to paycheck syndrome.
As interest accrued on my unpaid bills,
the only relief I got was from
dining in fine restaurants
and shopping in the best stores.
But, alas, symptomatic relief is not a cure.
My immune system was so compromised,
I came down with rubber checken pox.
After I recovered, the virus
remained in my system.
In later life it came back
as the painful kited check pestilence.

Now in my dotage, I feel the effects of
fixed income atrophy,
the result of cash flow hemorrhage.
I have just been diagnosed
with terminal financial embarrassment.
When I die, please lay me out quickly
before deadbeatamortis sets in.
On my tombstone have inscribed:
TOO BAD TO GO TO HELL*

*The monument maker will complain for the rest of his life
that he was stiffed by a stiff.

GIFTS

Once as a gift to my artist husband,
I gave a block of African wonder stone,
dark and dense.
I asked him what he would make of it.
I will carve, he replied,
and it will become a work of art.
The stone will tell me what to do.
Stone has its own life.
It makes its own statement.

Once as a gift my husband gave me
a <u>Websters New International Dictionary,</u>
replete with all the words and their nuances
of the English language.
He asked me why I wanted
so ponderous a lexicon.
I will write, I said.
The words will speak themselves,
and a poem will come into being.
Words have their own life.
They make their own statement.

KVELL*

You may have enjoyed watching
Michael Phelps win his eight gold medals.
What I enjoyed even more
was watching his mom, Debbie,
watching her son receive them.
There is a type of joy that
only mothers of Olympic

gold medalists can experience.
I know because I am one.

Every year before she competes
I stand next to my daughter
as she recites the
Special Olympics Oath,
Let me win, but if I cannot win,
let me be brave in the attempt.
Every year I take my place
in the bleachers of the
state university's natatorium
to cheer her on
in her three freestyle events.
This year she aced it,
three gold medals.

I propose there be a new Olympic event,
a *kvelling* contest for mothers of gold medalists.
Put me in the same heat as Debbie Phelps.
Place me in the lane next to hers.
When the gun goes off, so will we.
As we stand there glowing in the reflected glory
of our remarkable children, I will strive to win,
but if I cannot win, I will lose only
by one one-hundredth of a microwatt,
and I will be brave in the attempt.

YIDDISH: Uncontainable delight, conspicuous pride, most
commonly over the achievement of a child, especially one's
own.

NO ATHEISTS IN FOX HOLES

> *There are no Atheists in Fox Holes.*
> *~~Sermon delivered in the field, Bataan, 1942.*

Grandpa lived in the apartment above his dry goods store
in South Amboy, New Jersey.
He settled there after he left his native Ukraine
to escape from religious persecution,
a victim of oxymoronic history.

For his religion was no religion at all,
his creed, *There is no God.*
Labels that indicated God was worshiped
one way or another
were as meaningless to him as religion itself.
Worship, prayer? Comfort food
for feeble minds, he said.
Go to any house of the so-called God,
he told his children.
Nothing there but hypocrites and fools.
We will not join. We do not belong.

In another ironic twist,
his daughter, my mother, married a man
of the orthodox faith. Sabbath and holidays
were observed in our home.
At our Passover seder, when it was Grandpa's turn
to read from the Haggadah,
he read passionately in perfect Hebrew.
As he read, he seemed to be transported to a world
we would never know,
his own personal fox hole in the Ukraine,
one where he hid from his real enemies and his own demons
and waited for a Moses to take him to the promised land.

When he died, he was buried as he told my grandmother
he wished to be, in his best suit
and the skullcap and prayer shawl
that had been given to him at his bar mitzvah.
Grandpa had kept these through all the years
and all the migrations.
They were packed away in a drawer where he kept
his linen handkerchiefs, his silver cufflinks,
and his important papers.

It seems it doesn't matter what you call
the hole in the ground,
a foxhole, a grave.
If you're looking for an atheist,
you won't find one there.

SING THE BALLAD

Neither the cross of Jesus
nor the star of David
marks his tombstone.
It is the treble clef
that defines his brief life.
His epitaph reads,
Did I sing the ballad yet?
Was I wonderful?

Questions that beg the question,
why the questions?
What was the music of his life,
and what was the tale
he wanted to tell,

and did he ever tell it?
Was his epitaph his way of life,
or were these his last words,
a final statement on finality?
And what is my fascination with this anyway?

Will the music that fills my life
still be my soul's passion,
even when I can no longer hear it?
Will the story of my life
be a tale still told
even after I no longer live
in the events that made it?
Do I live my life as a ballad
that is to be sung by generations who follow me?
And is this how I will create
my own immortality?

Or will the music and the tale
die with me and pass
into the oblivion from which it came?
And as I'm carried to my grave
will I wonder and ask,
Did I sing the ballad yet?
Was I wonderful?

THE MATTER OF MY BOOK

I am myself the matter of my book.
~~Michel Equem de Montaigne, from his essay: To the Reader

Some people say you are what you eat.
But me, I am what I read.
As a child, I was every beautiful princess,

every damsel in distress
invented by the Brothers Grimm
and Hans Christian Anderson.
I was always rescued by the handsome prince,
and we always lived happily ever after.
I was as feisty as Gretel,
brave as Little Red Riding Hood,
positive as Pollyanna.
I was Nancy Drew, girl detective;
never left a case unsolved.
I was Nurse Nancy;
never lost a patient.

I grew to be, and so I am
the strength of Scarlet O'Hara,
never letting defeat defeat me.
I am Elizabeth Bennet and Jane Eyre,
able to gain acceptance, only on my own terms.
I am the loyalty of Antigone,
the passion of Molly Bloom.
I am Emily Gibbs' realization
of the value of life.
I am Virginia Woolf,
longing for a room of my own.

I am the universality of a Frost poem,
the humanity of a Shakespearean character,
the truth in humor of Mark Twain,
the beauty in simplicity of the Romantics.
I am the creation and embodiment
of every poet, playwright, and author
on my bookshelf.
I am myself the matter of my book;
I am what I read.

THE TENTH SYMPHONY

The dissonance of life before we met,
Like the first chord of his first symphony,
Prepared the way for our living duet,
Harmony brought forth from disharmony.
Beethoven's symphonies, nine in number,
Each one precursor for the one to come,
His progress forward unencumbered,
Obstacles to which he would not succumb.
We, too, forged on as fate knocked at our door,
Each other's hero as we chose rebirth,
Each other's shepherd, each other restore
Through exuberant dance, poetic mirth.
As the *Ode to Joy* that you've been to me,
So our *Ode to Love*, the tenth symphony.

WHALE SONG

And now, said our naturalist
aboard our whale watch vessel,
*I will drop a hydrophone
into the water, and you can hear
the song of the whales.*

At first all I heard was
a cacophony of random music,
but as I listened, I found myself
humming the quartet from *Rigoletto*
along with this oceanic choir.
For their music was neither random
nor cacophonous. It was purposeful,
haunting, magical.

In the sequences of howls and moans
I heard the trills of the soprano,
the sonorous tones of the tenor,
the booming of the bass.
Repeated themes resonated, and,
am I crazy, did I detect rhyme?
An opera of their own,
perhaps a drama of intrigue and anger.
But I did notice a touch
of opera bouffe, and was that
the improvised riff of the jazz musician?

How, I wonder, could I have been
so unaware in my limited perspective
as to think that only my species
could compose and perform
an operatic microcosm,
one that is larger than life?
I heard tales of love and lovers,
of hunters and the hunted,
written and performed by
cetaceous Verdis and Mozarts,
giants of the deep, their message
too deep for my shallow understanding.

WHEN FRANK PLAYS THE CLARINET

When Frank plays the clarinet,
he becomes the instrument,
perfect scale, rich sound,
mellow, mysterious.
Lost in the beauty of
the composer's virtuosity,

Frank bares his soul.
He is the music itself,
a clarinet concerto.
Confident, commanding,
He dares whole orchestras
to follow his theme.
And I, enchanted as a child
who follows the Pied Piper,
I become the instrument he plays,
the music itself,
a clarinet concerto, rich, mellow,
mysterious, perfect.

WITCHES' BREW

Round and round the oceans go,
in the putrid poisons throw.
Double, double, toil and trouble,
dolphins die and oceans bubble.

Mercury extracts, pcb's,
spoil the waters by degrees.
Tampon inserts, medical waste,
to melt a turtle's carapace.
To make the potion more desirous,
bacteria, morbillivirus,
Double, double, toil and trouble,
dolphins die and oceans bubble.

Radioactive toxic water,
ingredient of massive slaughter.
Pollutants, garbage, oil spills,
refuse of defiled landfills.

Biotoxins sewage bred,
emanate from watersheds.
Double, double, toil and trouble,
dolphins die and oceans bubble.

Pneumonias, ulcers, bites of sharks,
signs of suffering's watermark.
Witness dolphins' morbid event,
is this somehow God's intent?
Dolphonic requiem redefined,
as elegy for humankind.
Double, double, toil and trouble,
dolphins die and oceans bubble.

A DARK PREMONITION

"A crow just walked across my grave." That, my grandmother told me, was what someone would say in the old days in Russia if ever he had a dark premonition.

The yard of our house had many tall trees, the perfect nesting place for crows. One spring day I saw crows on the roof of our house. Out of nowhere I said to my husband, "Someone is going to die, someone important. I'm feeling New York." The next day we heard that John Cardinal O'Conner, Archbishop of New York, had died of cancer.

"How did you know?" my husband asked.

"A crow walked across my grave," I replied.

One month later I went to visit a family friend who was in a nursing home. Outside, scratching and cawing in a freshly dug flower bed, was a small flock of crows. "Mrs. Worth is going to die," I told my husband when I got home. Three weeks later, that was the case.

"What made you think she was going to die?" my husband asked.

"A crow walked across my grave," I said.

In the middle of a sultry summer we looked out into our atrium, the setting for a fish pond. A crow, feathers all ruffled, teetered on the edge of the rain gutter. "Who's going to die now?" my husband asked.

"The crow," I said to him. Then to the crow I said, "Go somewhere else to die." I left the room. When I returned, the crow was gone. That night there was a torrential rain storm. I thought I heard a loud splash, but it was, after all, a rain storm. The house was in the woods. Strange sounds in the night were not unusual.

After the storm I went out to clean debris from the pond. I never wore my glasses for this task. I saw what looked like a plastic garbage bag caught underneath overhanging plants. I reached with my hand to pull it out, then screamed as I brought into my range of vision a dead crow, all bedraggled feathers, red eye glaring at me. The crow had died, fallen into the storm gutter, was washed out in the rain storm, and then fell into the pond.

"West Nile virus," the man from animal control said.

My husband said, "You're giving me the creeps." It was one of the last conversations we had. Soon after that my husband suddenly died.

A few days ago, after hearing some dark news about myself, I felt compelled to visit him where he lies. In a voice that sounded more familiar than ever in the silence from which it came, he said, "I knew you would come today."

"How did you know?" I asked.

He answered, "A crow walked across my grave."

H. A. Maxson

DOG DREAMS

What does she dream, this black lab
stretched out on the floor in afternoon
sun, rear legs like pistons, sides
heaving as she gulps air?
                    What does she dream?
Fields? The beach? The weekend woods?
Her eyes do not betray her secret world,
her eyelids flutter but do not speak
of waves and sand or leafmold and trees.

She gallops through a world
I can only guess, perhaps forgets
before she wakes (like us). Or maybe
she remembers, relives those moments,
puzzles over them.
                Maybe that stare
is not so blank, maybe she runs the film
over and over and wonders how she
can be here on a rug in the sun
and not there in a field of snow,
or wet high grass, or on the beach
running full out between dunes and waves.

When I rose to fetch my notebook
I startled her awake. She rolled over
slowly, laid her head on crossed front paws.
She stared at me at the dining room table
writing down what might be her dream.

Laura McCullough

RADIATION

Stand on the sidewalk
with a cup of warm soup, curry,
the color of wheat in late August, and let yourself

be seen. It's the currency
of the street. Wear nothing
or everything you own. It doesn't matter. They'll devour

you with their eyes,
grateful for your humanity today.
What you see when you look back is the depth of space

behind each cheekbone,
the distance between the street
and an open window where sadness lurks in the shape

of a man who found
out today he can't have children.
His face is luminous, the color of curry or yarrow,

your finest eye shadow,
the one meant to capture autumn.
It's there in his eyes more beautiful than anything.

In the lot of the hardware
store someone watching
you sees the color of your brother's car accident

rolling off your shoulders
like heat off hot tar in July.
They recognize the smell of unresolved childhood

grief, and it fills them
the way good, yeasty bread does.
Let them look; you're busy. The man in the window

is stretching now,
his white chest wide, spine cracking
and with it the odor of vanilla ice cream on a good man's

beard when he kissed you
goodbye. Turn away, walk along
the brick curb radiating all the accrued sunshine you can

on the surface of your skin
like a body glove. Greet passersby
with a direct gaze. Be confident they see right through you.

If someone begins to cry,
tell them a few blocks down,
is a man in an open window with a chest like a snowy day.

D. J. Moores

THE PROBLEM OF RAPTURE IN THE LITERATURE CLASSROOM

Generally speaking, popular culture has been rather kind to teachers and professors of literature, who are often depicted in films as being inspiring, eccentric, and sagacious. John Keating, for example, the protagonist of the great film *Dead Poets Society*, is one such figure. Keating is an unorthodox freethinker who has been so moved to rapture from reading literature, especially Romantic poetry, that he teaches his students how to have a similar response not only to great texts but also to life itself. His repeated injunction, *carpe diem,* recurs throughout the movie and in some ways serves as its unifying theme. Although the film ends tragically, it seems safe to say that it casts Keating and his rapture in a positive light.

But the question remains whether this is the kind of thing that happens in a literature classroom. I suggest that at the undergraduate level, some professors—I don't know the percentages—teach literature in the way Keating does in *Dead Poets*, but they do so either apprehensively behind closed doors, within the confines of the classroom sanctuary (as I do), or, if they have tenure, they do so openly but to the chagrin and possibly even open disapproval of their peers.

I encountered hostility to Keating's approach recently at an academic literature conference I attended in the United Kingdom. In a breakout session on Walt Whitman, a colleague—a young, sophisticated scholar from one of the U.K.'s best schools—complained that when he teaches the poet his students begin to write and think like him. While some people, like myself, would see this as a mark of success, it signified a problem for my colleague, who saw it as a lyrical retreat into one's emotional confines and thus a distraction away from the deeper, more important concerns of his Marxist perspective and the ongoing class struggle it calls for.

This scholar, like so many others in literary studies, was likely influenced, whether directly or indirectly, by the work of Mikhail Bakhtin, whose brilliant ideas, particularly on the European Carnival tradition and the dialogic nature of literary language, I have used in my own work. Bakhtin's perspective on the lyric, however, is . . . well . . . not as productive. Bakhtin held a deep, Marxist distrust of the lyric because it is "in flight from history and the real." The form, he claimed, "is defined by a willful and permanent forgetting, an active refusal to allow the whole to be seen, and that part of the whole which is lost is the interaction of the world and the object over time, which has produced layers of supplementary or contradictory meaning." While his ideas are irresistibly interesting, Bakhtin's wholesale dismissal of the lyric is highly questionable because it denies the validity of an important literary form—the lyric, which can be apolitical but nonetheless opens a window into the limbic system (the emotional part of the brain) in a way that narrative does not.

So there is a disconnection between the image of the literature teacher/professor of popular culture and what actually goes on in a literature classroom, especially in the graduate seminar. I often hear from former students that graduate school is quite a drag, as it teaches them not how to love but how to resent and deconstruct the works that previously moved them to rapture. Attending graduate school from 1995-2003, I encountered and strongly resisted such an approach to literature, even dissolving my first doctoral dissertation committee out of frustration with my professors' critical orientations. This may sound a bit unusual to some but not to others who are familiar with the culture wars. In his brilliant work *The Western Canon,* Harold Bloom famously dubbed such a perspective the "school of resentment," as it represents a rejection of the call to rapture in favor of engaging in a "hermeneutics of suspicion." Such a form of reading literary texts has its origins in the work of three grandmasters of suspicion—Marx, Nietzsche, and Freud, some of the most gifted and influential thinkers of the modern period. Literature professors who employ suspicion as a form of interpretation typically elide the surface of the text in favor of some obscured depth. In this sense, they are more concerned not with what the text says and the rapture it may prompt on the surface but what it conceals. This obscured ugliness is usually either psychopathology, as in neurosis or psychosis, or objectionable ideology, whether patriarchal, heterosexist, racist, bourgeois, or imperialist. Such a form of reading is immensely valuable, as it has given birth to the rich, rigorous tradition known as critical theory, which has, in the last thirty years, immeasurably enriched literary and cultural studies in numerous ways. But surely there are other ways of reading! Even Paul Ricoer, the French scholar who coined the term, "hermeneutics of suspicion," also noted that it is but one possible reading strategy, not the grand narrative it has become. Ricoer also coined the phrase "hermeneutics of affirmation" to designate ways of reading that do not employ suspicion as a primary concern and instead read with the grain, affirming what the textual surface suggests rather than eliding it as a symptom of some underlying psychopathology or ideological complicity.

I say all of this as someone who loves and continues to read the work of Nietzsche, Marx, and Freud but who also stands opposed to fundamentalism of all kinds, even sophisticated versions that reduce the complexities of the rapturous response to complex literature to false consciousness or psychological disease. So as to avoid being called a reactionary or a political conservative, let me further clarify my own ideological position: I write all of these comments as a left-leaning, alternative-minded, neo-hippie who lives in southern California and regularly attends all-night drum and dance circles and alternative festivals such as Burning Man. I am extremely sensitive to and supportive of gay people, women, people of color, immigrants, and anyone marginalized. In fact, I have a blood relation in every one of such categories. I recently joined the "Million-Mask March" in London, where Anonymous protesters decried the excesses of the uber-rich. Given my own values, I, too, live on the margins and identify as a fringe-dweller. So when I say *with vehemence* that there are more ways to read a work of literature than to deconstruct it as a symptom of jaundiced psychology or objectionable ideology, I do so, however ironic it may be, as someone who sympathizes strongly with the political forces the school of suspicion actually claims to represent. I, too, am a lefty, but I am not so politically entrenched that I cannot question the assumptions of other left-wingers. To the contrary, I always question.

This suspicious approach that denies the text's rapture was born out of the sixties ferment and the New Left it spawned, according to Terry Eagleton, himself a Marxist scholar. By the end of that decade, Nixon and a number of unfortunate events (Altamont, Kent State, the Manson murders, the illegalization of psychedelics, etc.) effectively killed the protest movements on the streets, the result of which was that scholars in literary studies began to use this same spirit of protest against the texts that for centuries had been deemed canonical and thus worthy of great respect. Of course, sexism, heterosexism, racism, and imperialism do exist in so many texts of the past, but that is simply to say that older generations and the writers they influenced cannot measure up to contemporary benchmarks of political correctness; it does not mean that being moved to rapture or some other affective response implicates the reader in neuroticism or imperialism. And it also does not mean that a rapturous response to such texts is wrong, detrimental, or misguided. To the contrary, powerful affective responses and the states of flow we enter when engaging a complex literary text are, according to contemporary neurology, psychology, and even some literary scholars, immeasurably valuable as a means to enhance one's well-being. Try to imagine being happy in a colorless world in which there was no such thing as beauty. Being powerfully moved by beauty is something that makes life worth living.   Surely, it is more than a political retreat or symptom of neurosis.   I can't emphasize this enough because to speak of literature as though it is an object of beauty capable of moving us to rapture, according to so many of my suspicious peers, is considered either fallacious or a sign that one is not politically aware.   And that, I suggest, is a crude reduction.

The intelligent but non-academic reader already knows that literature should not be so crudely reduced to ideology and that rapture is important, without knowledge of the debates in literary and cultural studies.   A good example of this can be seen in what I have called the "Rumi phenomenon."   In the last thirty years, translations of Rumi, a thirteenth-century Sufi poet, have sold somewhere around thirty million volumes in the Anglophone world, while even prize-winning poets do well if they sell 10,000 volumes in a given year.   Why has Rumi become so popular 800 years after he lived?   A partial answer to this question is that his poetry fills the void left by the Western turn away from traditional religion towards a kind of churchless, gnostic spirituality that Rumi's Sufism, at least in the versions selling in the Western world, represents.   Another part of the answer is that Rumi is an ecstatic poet who intended his verse to lift readers into ecstatic states of consciousness, into rapture.   To read Rumi ideologically or psychodynamically, then, is to miss the point entirely, as he intended his verse to serve as a catalyst to rapture, which his affirmative readers know all too well.

For all of this disconnect, the times they are a-changin'.   At the turn of this century, there was a radical shift in psychology, the result of the laudable work of Martin Seligman, currently the world's most frequently cited psychologist.   In 1998, Seligman used his tenure as the president of the American Psychological Association to catalyze a transformation in his discipline, which, at that point, was almost solely focused on disease and psychopathology. Now, after the influence of Seligman and others, thousands of psychologists around the world are researching what many consider to be the most important of all human concerns— well-being. This type of eudaimonic or "positive" psychology is concerned not merely with the mitigation of disease and the easing of suffering—which, despite some notable exceptions, more or less describes the first one hundred years of psychology as a discipline—but with the question of what it means to be well in the fullest sense, to thrive. Since then, this fecund concern with well-being has overgrown disciplinary lines and even crept into and taken root in other fields of study. Today, historians, sociologists, economists, architects, political scientists, business professors, neurologists, and many other scholars have cultivated a deep concern with this question. A general search on the term "well-being" in the EBSCO research database yields around 300,000 hits. It seems that human flourishing has become more than a casual interest in academe. To the contrary, in the past decade especially, it has become something of a multidisciplinary preoccupation.

This new concern with what it means to be well, which James Pawelski and I have called "the eudaimonic turn" in a volume by the same name, has also found expression, albeit it in an indirect way, in literary studies. The inquisitorial hyper-vigilance that had become synonymous with literary and cultural theory from the seventies onward has been, in the last few years, increasingly called into question. Just as scholars of suspicion challenged and ultimately supplanted the New Critics of the mid-twentieth century, so have younger scholars in recent years answered the literary establishment's focus on psychopathology and undesirable ideology with what has been called "affirmative reading," "literal reading," "positive aesthetics," "surface reading," and the like. The younger generation has become suspicious of suspicion. This new trend of reading with the grain and rejecting what Peter Barry has called "textual harassment," actually began with the later work of a brilliant scholar of suspicion, Eve Sedgwick, who nevertheless called for a new, "reparative" way of reading in a now famous and influential essay, "Paranoid Reading and Reparative Reading: or, You're so Paranoid, You Probably Think This Introduction is about You." Here, Sedgwick suggests that suspicion, taken to extremes, is itself diseased and can become a kind of unfounded paranoia, claiming that there are other ways of reading in which we might *repair* our relationship to the text. Recent scholars such as Rita Felski, Heather Love, Sharon Marcus, Stephen Best, and others, have taken Sedgwick's cue, calling old-style critique into question and even claiming, as Bruno Latour does, that it has "run out of steam." A newer set of loosely related approaches, all of which are being referred to as "surface reading," has taken root and begun to blossom in literary studies. The *surface* of such reading strategies is, contrary to its name, not simple surface in any sense but a return to the aspects of the text that were previously deemed "mere surface" or "symptom" of something underlying and undesirable. On this surface are the enduring ethical questions, the emotions and other forms of affect, the human imagination, artistic skill (if not genius), and, perhaps most important of all, authorial ideas about what it means to be well, to flourish.

At this year's Modern Language Association convention, the premier conference for literary scholars, surface reading was more or less the central topic of debate. Of course, it is hotly contested, as the subject represents what is likely to be a generational turn, which of course entails the rejection or modification of entrenched critical positions and frequently used methods in literary studies. Of course, only time will tell where such a new way of reading will take us.

For all its promise, it is not likely that surface reading will eventually make commonplace the practice of having students stand on desks and howl at the full moon in between chanting lines from Whitman. Old ideas die hard and sometimes never really die. Music critics say the band Nirvana killed the heavy metal of the eighties, and yet Black Sabbath had a world tour and a number one album in 2013. Similarly, in the seventies suspicion supplanted the close reading of New Criticism as an approach to texts, and yet nearly every literary scholar today, regardless of methodology, uses this close reading strategy to some extent. I suspect suspicion will be a part of the critical landscape for many years to come, but these years will also see the growth of newer, affirmative reading strategies that will decenter suspicion as a master narrative. Yes, I think we have a long way to go before rapture is again acceptable in academe. But, I am not waiting with bated breath. And I will still try to get students, if not on their desks, at least on their feet as they sound their rapturous, barbaric yawps—full moon permitting, of course.

Sources: M. M. Bakhtin and P. N. Medvedev, *The Formal Method in Literary Scholarship,* trans. A. J. Wehrle, (Baltimore, Md.: Johns Hopkins University Press, 1978); Harold Bloom, *The Western Canon: The Books and School of the Ages* (New York: Riverhead, 1994); Paul Ricoeur, *Freud and Philosophy: An Essay on Interpretation* (New Haven, Conn.: Yale University Press, 1970); Amira El-Zein, "Spiritual Consumption in the United States," *Islam & Christian-Muslim Relations* 11.1 (2000); James Pawelski and D. J. Moores, eds., *The Eudaimonic Turn: Well-Being in Literary Studies* (Madison, N.J.: Fairleigh Dickinson University Press, 2013); Peter Barry, *Beginning Theory: An Introduction to Literary and Cultural Theory* (New York: Manchester University Press, 1995); Eve Kosofsky Sedgwick, "Paranoid Reading and Reparative Reading: or, You're so Paranoid, You Probably Think This Introduction is about You" in *Novel Gazing: Queer Readings in Fiction,* ed. Eve Kosofsky Sedgwick (Durham, N.C.: Duke University Press, 1997); Rita Felski, *The Limits of Critique* (Chicago: University of Chicago Press, 2015);

Heather Love, "Close but not Deep: Literary Ethics and the Descriptive Turn," *New Literary History* 41.2 (2010): 371-91; Stephen Best and Sharon Marcus, "Surface Reading: An Introduction," *Representations* 108 (Fall 2009): 1-20; Bruno Latour, "Why Has Critique Run Out of Steam? From Matters of Fact to Matters of Concern," *Critical Inquiry* 30.2 (2004): 225-48.

Anna Moran

I was born in County Tyrone Ireland, and came to America when I was sixteen.

I have always had a love affair with words. In Ireland being able to sing, write a poem, or tell a story was considered a gift.

When I was in my thirties I joined a poetry group in Rutherford N.J. It was affiliated with Farleigh Dickenson University. My work was published in the college magazine. Mark S. Germaine took the work of our group and set it to music. It played Off Off Broadway and was titled RIB. And more recently two of my poems were published in *"Ireland's Own" a Dublin Magazine,* also *Spindrift* and *Exit 13.* I am now a member of Jersey Shore Poets, and I find it a wonderful place to grow as a poet.

THE NIGHT STAND

What's on the nightstand lamp?
Two strands of red hair,
taped inside of the shade
for later show and tell.

In a restaurant booth
well past midnight,
four women talk about husbands.
Women share
a lot; an awful lot.

Pretty petite blond
in her thirties,
two children, a husband, a house.
Now on a journey to South Carolina:
to meet a stranger;
to commit adultery;
to get even
for the red hair
found in her husband's jockey shorts.

AN IRISHMAN'S THOUGHTS

An Irishman carries his soul in his heart,
and his home in his head;
at least, that is my way.
I carry my soul in my heart
and my house in my head,
and both will perish if I am not careful.

It is a balancing act:
God and Ireland.
Both demand fierce love;
and then, there is that place on the map
where one was born.
It's called "the home place."
It's securely ensconced in my head.

Memories paper the walls of its rooms.
Reality does not hold much quarter;
like an erector set, it builds upon itself:
Hurts are its flagstone floor;
the future its windows;
the roof its limits.

Then, there are the words:
words, words, words;
so many, many words:
thicker than flies;
sweeter than baby kisses;
more bitter even than death.

I left them all there.
Never got to sort them out.
They would not fit in my suitcase,
so they stayed in the home place
locked away like disgrace.
The new owner does not know they are there.
I dug them deep within stonewalls.

TWILIGHT

I became conscious beside him
earlier in the day.
I remembered his gaze upon me
and the awe I felt
as I beheld his beauty.

"My lovely one," he whispered
"You are part of me."

Now it is evening.
All is hushed,
even the earth forgets to breathe

As we lie together
He lavishes kisses
And smothered words of love
upon my eager body.

Oh wondrous man!
What feelings you awake in me
I trill as your fingers trail downward.

I have no fear.
Rejection!
Morning coldness!
Thoughts of escape!

It would be later
Much, much later
I would discover my nakedness
And weep with madness by the Euphrates.

A COUNTRY EVENING

There is nothing more satisfying
on a dark winter night
than to know
there is a bucket of cold spring water
next to a crock of fresh cream
in the scullery,
and a crackling turf fire on the hearth.

Hear the murmur of the wind,
the low of the cattle,
and the quiet stirring of hens on their roosts,
and a gentle soft silence
punctuated by the tumble of turf on the fire.

After the rosary, we'd sit and talk,
discuss the day in leisurely detail
and, as the silence deepened,
stories would be told
embroidered by night textures.

Footsteps, ghostly, evil in intent,
would be listened for with straining ear.
Desperate cries from the nether world
would be given life.
My brother and I would sit terror enthralled.

Then, bed.
I always dreaded bed.
Mother's haunted words carried their imagery,
lined the walls of my bedroom.
I scarce could breathe
except to beg my brother to keep talking
until I fell asleep.

However, that never stopped us
from wanting more and more stories.
It was a time of life that was peaceful and kind;
and, would that it could have lasted forever.

MY MOTHER'S BROKEN HEART

The bits and pieces of my mother's broken heart
became easy to see.
When some thought or word
caused her to remember,
her mind would touch the thought gently
probing as a doctor probes for pain.

It did not matter that her mother had just died,
with her arms wrapped tightly around her darling Mary.
They pried little Mary loose despite her tearful protest
that mammy was only sleeping.

A neighbor woman moved with pity,
took the sobbing four year old out of the chaos,
and brought her to her home.
She took the child to her bed that night
in a vain attempt to comfort her;
held her close to not avail.

Then, suddenly , in that dark, sad night
two arms reached across the bed
and lifted the sobbing child.
This unseen presence held her until she fell asleep;
then, laid her gently on the floor.

As soon as daybreak came,
Mary was brought back home.
"Keep her Packey, your dead wife wants
her with her father, not with old Mary and Tom;
they will be cruel to her,"
the neighbor pleaded.
Unfortunately, for my mother,
the living did not listen to the dead.

THE HOME PLACE

I still longed for my home place,
even, after the homesickness had passed.
The place where I first set tottering feet on
a flagged floor scrubbed clean with lye soap.

I go back in my mind's eye seeking my past.
But another question tugs at my soul,
"What are you really seeking?
Surely, not a piece of ground,
a house now occupied by others
who would but grudgingly lend you
a moment in their home.
It would not matter to them
that you were born there,
The ownership is now theirs
and, they would be threatened by your
need of the place."

So I go in my mind's eye
unobtrusively to the back room,
to the bed with its grey and white striped
mattress stuffed with straw,

covered in sun-bleached sheets
and feel again my mother's birth labor,
and the soft voice of the nurse coaxing her
through the pain until I came forth.

Not just from an earthly womb,
not just into temporary consciousness,
but, from another place.
And, that is what I discovered:
That other home place.
The door was closed to me then
but, beneath the silt of life, it purrs.
It purrs endlessly like a contented kitten
waiting patiently for me to come to awareness:
"That yes, that is where truly dwells my home place."

NIGHT TIME

Dusk has slipped away
taking mystical softness from my hills.
Gentle as a pansies touch,
night greets me.

The hand of man has turned
the clock back to its natural rhythm.
Earth, this autumn evening
has reclaimed her time.
We celebrate.

The hens are fed and roosted.
The cow has her hay.
The cat her milk,
and, the dog his dinner.

Night's pleasant darkness invites me
to do nothing but watch the flames curl
heavenward in the hearth
and; later, I slip quietly to bed.

There, I lie awake and listen
as the night and its sounds
wraps itself around me and
I respond and sink blissfully
within the darkness.

THE WHINNE BRAE

Running till the wind was out-of-ye,
bare legs brushing the tall grass.
The smell of honeysuckle and heather filling my lungs.

Running,
Screaming,
Laughing,
Cowboys and Indians
Weapons of stick guns
Sally rod bow and arrows.

Tossing ourselves with reckless abandonment
on our "dead" enemy.
"Lie still," I'd scream,
"I shot you through the heart."

"You missed," he'd giggle and push me off
and run away yelling and whooping,
one lone turkey feather stuck in his hair.

Gone as yesterday's river water,
gone as summer,
gone as night.

Oh! brother, beloved brother
how I wish
that you had never been shot.

A POEM

A poem is dangerous.
It has a life of its own.
It exists in the mind
and holds with words
the heart of the seeker,
and carries it down
roads not thought of.

Only the heart knows
it wants to be there,
because its dimensions
are not set in the ordinary;
but, defined by the giver.

Thoughts deform walls,
exposes them as ugly,
cause them to crumble.
It is the gift of the giver
to the one who wants
but does not know
with certainty, what?

A poem lives.
Its words:
companion the joyous and
the broken.
Its thoughts
make mental milestone.

A poet sings in the market place
even, when stoned.
Poets belong to God.

ANSWERED PRAYER

> *"More tears are shed over answered prayers than*
> *unanswered ones"*~~ *Truman Capote*

I had always wanted to eat in a fine dining
room stocked with silver, china, and fine linen.
We ate at the kitchen table with thick legs
and a top, scrubbed smooth as glass.

Then, one day, I sat at a grand dining table.
There was no mistaking its grandeur.
The linen was crisp, white, well ironed:
no tell tale wrinkles.
Silver, gleaming glass, and china in abundance.
There was even a smiling, obsequious waiter thrown in.

However, my heart was green with pain.
Nothing or no one was familiar.
Nothing, I could reach out and touch.
I longed for the warmth and feel of the cow's breath
on my fingers; the cackle of hens as they raced for
their food; my old dog, safe in the byre.

The grandeur of this floating palace mocked me.
This was not what I'd envisioned.
My mother and brothers sat across from me;
their blank faces reflected my shock.
Around us the sea roared and swelled, the wind blew,
and I sat and choked on the answer to my prayers.

A POWERFUL THING

He approached me hesitantly, "Do you have one? "

"Could I have a page, just one page?" he was thrilling with fear, looking furtively about him, as he asked the question in heavy accented English.

Somehow the word had gotten out that I had one; that I was not a casual tourist.

Miraculously, it had slipped through security; and now, here I was faced with a decision on this pebbled street, rimmed in poverty. "One page would be enough," he said. "You see our teacher was taken away because he told us about it. He did not have one himself but he told us about it."

The power that this book held was so unbelievable that just a page would relieve his hunger. How dangerous to the powers to be, that to own just one page would be enough to warrant arrest, flogging, even death. Its power was impervious to restraint. Now, I was the one afraid. Now my eyes searched the empty street for shadows. Now I wondered if someone was watching. However, I could not refuse. Unlike him, I only risked a few days in jail; then, expulsion: not death.

I reached inside my shirt and slipped it out of its hiding place. His eyes filled with joy. He grasped my hands in wordless gratitude, then scampered away clutching his treasure.

It is called, "The Living Word of God." It breathes life into dark places. It speaks of a power beyond that which exists in the here and now. It makes the impossible possible. Its miracles are commonplace. It breathes wisdom into those who ponder its words. It does not require great learning. Its ways are simple; yet, deadly effective. It has toppled dictators, and despots, and evil government: "deadly and fearful, indeed!"

DANGEROUS INDIFFERENCE

He came in the door carrying the tapestry in his arms. This foolish man was so happy. He thought the great bolt of cloth would please the woman he was foolish enough to fall in love with.

Oh! Dear friends, love is blind. But the most blind is the woman who is loved by a man who does not cause her pulse to race, or her heart to pound in pleasure at the sound of his voice.

Dangerously blind.

At the sight of him, she stifles a yawn, "Oh! The dumb ox;" her eyes say as she rolls them up to the ceiling. Meanwhile, her husband's sweat has turned cold, as he senses her displeasure.

"I thought you wanted a tapestry. I looked long and hard for it in all the shops on Fifth Street. See! It has the notes we danced to at our wedding woven into the tune the harpist is playing."

"See, it even has your favorite shades of red and orca woven in the sunset. Honey, darling I have tried so hard to please you. Why can't I? Why, you pay more attention to the garbage collector than you do to me.

Still stretched on the sofa, she mutters words of discontent unaware that her husband has raised the tapestry above her and brings it crashing down on her head.

"I will tell the police I dropped it," he mutters to himself, with a smile.

Patrick Moran

Patrick Moran was born in the Bronx of Irish Immigrant parents. Served in the Air Force for four years. Has BA and MA Degrees. He was a computer salesman 23 years and a high school teacher for 21 years, and never wrote poetry until he retired. He has found it to be a new, refreshing experience and fascinating in that he is learning to discover and share himself in entirely new ways.

DEAR MR. BALD HEAD

"Where did you come from and why did
you do this to me? You strangled my hairs,
closed the pores before they even turned
gray. How cruel! How deliberate! How mean!

How old was I? Barely out of high school
and there you came attacking a young
innocent kid, with no consideration of the
pain and angst you were putting me through.

What did I do wrong, Mr. Bald Head? So I
copied Tony Curtis' hairstyle as did so, so
many others. Yet, so many of my contemps
seem to have thriving gray manes of hair.

You should be ashamed, Mr. Bald Head.
Now, don't quote the Bible and refer to God,
who numbers all the hairs on our heads and
pretend you were making it easier for God."

"Mom, show me again that picture of your
dad. Look! He was bald, wasn't he?" "Thanks
so much, grandpa. I needed those genes of
yours so, so badly." "Oh, wait a minute here!"

"Mr. Bald Head, now you're blaming my poor
grandpa, whom I never met: the poor guy.
First, you robbed him and now it's my turn.
Boy! You are such a mean, dirty bastard."

THE CAR IN THE DRIVEWAY

"Will the car be in the driveway,"
I ask myself as I head home.
When not there, the house might as well
be a empty factory building.

"Darn," my spirit would cry,
disappointment
descending on me like a
heavy theatre curtain.

I would dread opening the door
with no "Hi Babes" to hear
and no "Hey Rooney girl"
to shout in response.

The car in the driveway is far more
than a make, year and model.
The car represents so many things:
a bond, a commitment. a promise, a history;

A life so precious and special
that only when that car is in the
driveway,
am I truly home.

TRUTH AND THE BEACH

It was a hot August day
and this Jersey beach was packed,
barely a spot to put your
beach chair and umbrella.

The ocean was warm and calm,
not crashing on the sand,
but quietly breaking ever
so gently on sun kissed bodies.

A lot of watching was going on:
mothers watching children,
men watching the bikini clad
mothers.

One pensively watching
all the activity and wondering,

"If one swam laterally across this
expanse, where would he arrive?"
and then, "How does one know the
globe on which he found the
answer was correct?"

We often believe others with reservation:
the bad doctor, the good doctor,
the honest politician, the dishonest one,
Darwinist scientists, Intelligent Design
believers.

Globe makers make believing so
much easier; but then again, "Would
it still be Portugal in—say, '2075'
when one of us finishes her swim?"

WHAT ARE ORDINARY THINGS, ANYWAY?

Get dressed, undressed. Pick up a book to read or a newspaper
    or magazine.
Answer the phone or make a peanut butter sandwich. Pour
    a glass or water, juice or wine. Wash hands, shower, or
towel oneself dry.
    Hear and watch a plane roar in the overhead sky to leave its
contrails behind and to think of its people inside going
        somewhere
    to do something.

All ordinary things.

To see a dead squirrel, or possum or gopher by the side of the
    highway or spot a family of deer swiftly jump in front of you
as they cross the wooded road.
    To walk into a spider web outside your front door or hear
the sound of katydids in the trees above.
    To observe the rabbits on the bike trail as they stop, eye
you and hop calmly into the adjoining woods.

All ordinary things

A mother pushing a child in a stroller. A man walks his dog
    with his bag of dog poop in his hand.
Hunched backed, skinny cyclists on their thin wheeled bikes
    wear their uniforms of black helmets, tight shorts, colorful
        tees.
Harleys with mufflers saying "We're here!" as they assault all ears
    with their snorts, rumbles and bellows.
Teen age boys' shouts, girls' giggles, workmen loudly bark
    orders.

All ordinary things

Some things are always with us, seen, heard, felt and provoke
    little response. There is a special panache and peace in
        ordinary
things for they are only recognized in ordinary times.

ASSIGNMENT: IWO

First, San Antonio for basic; then, Cheyenne for technical training;
    now,
    School was over. The bulletin board posted our assignments.
Air Force life was finally beginning.

    I scanned the wall sheet: Germany, France, England, Germany
        again and again,
"Here I am!" I fingered and said audibly, "Iwo Jima! What the hell!
    The story of my life!" I continued to myself, "What the hell is Iwo
        Jima and where is It? A big battle was fought there but what's
        there?" Sands and John Wayne came immediately to mind.

"What in heaven's name am I going to do on Iwo Jima?" I bellowed.
    The other guys all seemed to giggle and immediately lost interest
as they shared their excitement wondering what famous European city
    they would be near.

Again, I felt totally out of it.
    Bad enough, the Air Force made a clerk typist out of me;
now, I would be a clerk typist on a miniature island
    somewhere in the Pacific.

What would I tell my folks? No diploma after four years of high school,
    they paid for.

I joined the Air Force to serve my country, to do something to redeem
    myself.
    My parents and six siblings were waiting for word from the "Black
    Sheep" youngest.

They would be numb when I told them, particularly my Irish born
    parents,
    who, maybe, never even heard of the place.
I already felt the humiliation of my announcement overwhelm me:
    like being
    covered totally by a thick, black woolen robe.

The five by two mile island met expectations:
    Black volcanic sand tortured feet.
Shark fins in ocean destroyed any notion of swimming or even wading.
    Pool fungus rendered base pool off-limits.
Never any relief from the heavy, salt-laden air and drenching sweat.

I had a fruitful experience though: new friendships, great outdoor
    movie theatre and 45 pounds of muscle added to my
    scarecrow frame.
Developed my desire to get GED and go to college.
    Read Russian authors: Tolstoy, Dostoevsky, Chekov and also Ayn
    Rand's books.
Favorite character, by far, was Prince Myshkin of Dostoevsky's
    <u>The Idiot.</u>
    I found me in that character and also on Iwo Jima, itself.

LIFE IS WORTH LIVING

Melodious sound waves carrying Beethoven's Fifth
    fill air, intoxicate ears, calm very being.
His notes of music originating in his mind have similarly
    affected many listeners through the centuries.

Even every person's speaking voice can challenge
    mind, dazzle, provoke questions of how, why.
Similarly, shouts, cries, whispers, all one's own
    as are intonations, pitches, of each voice.

Distinctive walk, run, skip, accompanying
    arm swing movement, all definitely personal;
as is every sweep of the floor, swing
    of a bat, shovel or carry of a package.

Fingerprints identifying you as a person,
    are as mysterious as complex DNA: yours alone
and different from the billions and billions
    of others before and to come after you.

We are wonderfully made says the Sage and
    as unique as snowflakes are to each other.
Yet, we didn't make ourselves though we can
    transform ourselves or be transformed.

Life is worth learning about our specialness,
    our intelligence, our beauty, our creativity,
our ability to feel, empathize, make decisions
    to love, hate, reject or grow in wisdom.

Many, many, have testified to a post-life world
    where a more aware consciousness prevails
and a more perfect creation exists. Logic and
    reason suggests there is never an end to learning.

MY FIRST LOVE

I would go by her window with the "Street Where You
        Live" lyrics swimming sweetly in my head.
"Would she come to the window," I would wonder and
        then glance once and then again, hoping for a miracle.
She didn't come, never did, though I walked down her
        block many, many times hoping and dreaming

"Flo likes you," said her fourteen year old friend
        earlier and that was all I needed for I always envied
my friend Don for his girlfriend: Flo.
        Surprisingly, he broke off with her after months
but it took her but weeks, before she dumped me.

I was devastated by the experience; for I loved the
        spirit and energy that radiated from her
and, of course, her soft full breasts; but perhaps,
        I reflected my caring too much.

She wasn't particularly pretty. I guess attractive
        would be a more suitable word, but she was
a big "IT" for me: Her laugh was from her belly.
        She smiled all the time and her body was soft
and warm to my touch.
        My fourteen year old heart was split into a hundred
pieces by the sudden end of the relationship.

John, her sixteen year old boyfriend—before Don,
        wanted her back and she him.
Ironically, her boyfriend's sister, Joan, much,
        much prettier than Flo, liked me. It is not looks
I discovered at fourteen that makes the difference;
        but, the way you affect others.

Florence Klein, my first love, my first exposure
    to the fair sex, ignited me, enthralled me and
captured my heart.

THE POWER OF A DREAM

Whenever I see people jogging in the streets,
I remember that I ran for over twenty years.
Whatever the weather, nothing kept my
Saucony running shoes and I from the pavement.

The young women can't be stopped any more than
their long pony-tailed hair flopping side to side
can be, as they amble along. All of them remind me
of my runner daughter Mary's bouncing blond hair.

All ages of men and women pound the sidewalks,
roads, bicycle paths but mostly adults, young and
middle aged as I was when I started at forty. And I
imagine I was like those big guys I see with the
clodhopper strides.

They talk of a runner's high and it is a very real thing.
Endorphins flood your brain making you feel so! so! good.
And why not, you're doing something wonderful for
yourself, your heart, your waistline, and your pride.

But what really propels you onward is that dream
to join the thousands of others challenging themselves
to achieve faster and faster times and to run longer and
longer races.

Every serious runner knows what is meant by "The Half."
It is a prelude to "The Big One": the 26.2 mile Marathon.
There were 25,000 dreamers who finished with me in 1986.
My daughter was one of 45,000 finishing her recent New York.

We reached for the gold and did it;
and, collected a medal to remind us always
that a dream, a hope, a plan has great unimaginable power.

Mihaela Moscaliuc

HOW TO ASK FOR MY HAND AT MY GRANDMOTHER'S GRAVE

"What a waste of space," you murmur as the train cuts
through a cemetery whose halves rest like drowsy wings
between two pine forests, then "spooky" as our window
zips by faces smiling from porcelain plates glued to crosses.
You've crossed the ocean to marry me, so I cannot say
    I knew only one of them, but they are all mine,
    these dead turned strigoi who'll not return
    to their bodies because the earth's too loud
    and the town has betrayed them.
But I have to warn you—
    We carry cemeteries on our heads,
    in our bellies, round our ankles,
    we carry them to work
    and we carry them to sleep
    and when we make love
    they moan, they rattle, they sing.
    When our spine starts sinking we spit
    and curse and dance the pain off.
When I bring you to Grandmother's grave,
behind the Dacian fortress, she'll be armed
with questions: how hardy your love, how soft your fingers,
and your dead, how do you spoil them?
"After you cup your hands to catch the soul,"
she'll want to know, "how do you release it?"
Don't tell her about ashes thrown to winds, don't say
you've never spilled red wine onto the earth
to quench your father's thirst, or that you never read to him
the Sunday paper. Do not tell her you love him
but have never seen his grave. I'll translate your silence

and spread a white cloth under the rose trellis. We'll offer
walnut breads and gossip, and she'll forgive, and bless us,
then send me back across the ocean with a saddlebag of ghosts.

Linda Johnston Muhlhausen

Linda Johnston Muhlhausen writes in a variety of genres and over the years has published poems, poetry book reviews, short fiction, essays, and creative non-fiction. Her poetry has appeared in *Thema, The Writer, Whirlwind Magazine, Howl of Sorrow, This Broken Shore*, with poetry book reviews in *American Poetry Review, Pittsburgh Poetry Review* and *Pleiades.* She believes that poetry is witness, wonder, catharsis, and sometimes as sensual as making love in the dark.

Linda was born on Long Island, New York, and received a Bachelor's degree in English from State University of New York at Binghamton in 1971. After graduation, she joined the U.S. Peace Corps and traveled to Uganda, East Africa, where she taught English Language and Literature at an all-boys secondary school until evacuated from the country in fall of 1972. She wrote a novel, loosely based on this experience, as yet unpublished.

In 2012, she earned a Master's Degree in English, concentration in Creative Writing, from Monmouth University. She is chairperson of the Monmouth County Fiction Writer's Guild critique group, a member of Jersey Shore Poets critique group, and co-host of the River Read Reading Series in Red Bank, N.J. She is employed as a contributing editor for a lifestyle magazine and administrative assistant for Red Bank Chamber Music Society. Linda has two adult daughters and lives in Middletown, N.J.

ANEURYSM

for Felix, "the Music Man"

This is how it ends:

First,
slick bubble
swells,
slow bulb
tests membrane,
tender tissue
worn thin,
frail as feather.

Then,
slim lipped
fissure widens,
mouth taken
by surprise:
hole gapes,
gulf stream gushes.
No failsafe
dam, dike
to hold back
your life's
bright oil—

Last,
surgeon rushes
from ninth hole,
mops brow,
glasses slipping.
Scrubs—
too late!

Your song
bleeds out
past clamps,
sutures,
hurried hands—
          your silver music,
          this bronze river.

MY OTHER EAR

> *I wanna sleep with you in the desert tonight*
> *with a billion stars all around*
> ~~"Peaceful Easy Feeling," the Eagles

While other girls dream Eagles' love songs, starry skies,
I think—snakes.

While for faithful fourteens, Shea is Beatle Mecca,
I think—stampede.

While thousands flock to Woodstock rock,
I think mud, shit—hepatitis.

While others make love without rings,
I think—marriage.

While we camp nude at Empire Lake,
I think—sunburnt nipples.

While it rains on our spaghetti,
I think—hunger.

While sheltered in the car with cake and merlot
I think—suffocation.

While daughters grow and we implode,
I think—shrapnel.

While the blue loveseat mocks me,
I think—I hate—your recliner.

While I eat cherries from a cracked crystal bowl
I think—slivers.

When I walk in our desert and see a spring
I think—mirage.

While we make love once more for old time's sake
I think—sand. How it runs out through the fingers.

PECTUS EXCAVATUM

The sunken chest of grade school
breast jokes touched my secret
rib cage deformity   scooped concavity
benign hollow where bone bends
its curved-in cage & heart bumps
its soft fist against the bars,
beat, beat   & beat
its syncopation bravely borne
its life sentence cramped captivity
heart & I ignore

& so the mind cocoons the self
& so the self   minds its store
wraps its fragile pear or peach
& packs it in excelsior

SEUSSED FOREVER

One fish or two, red, or blue,
These are conundrums that get to you
In rollicking rhythm and gamboling rhyme
Infesting the heart and mind over time,

But whatever my weak spot, the heart or the mind
It's a wonderfully awe-ful thing to find
That at this late date there's no getting loose:
I'm totally hooked on Dr. Seuss.

My daughters two are now immune
To his scrumptiously bumptious, crafty cartoons
Too busy with this, too busy with that
To spend any time with a cat in a hat.

That may seem all wrong but it's really all right
They must see the world, fight the good fight
So much to do, oh the places they'll go
To walk their own paths, but I'll always know

Those comfortable moments when their little feet
Were tucked in all warm under blanket and sheet
The books of their choice all brought into bed,
And I read what they wanted—I read and I read

'Til my head was spinning, my throat was sore
And I thought I could never read one story more
As they begged and pleaded, I ooblecked and grinched
Unleashing those words like a worm that inched

Its way into *my* tired brain, growing stronger
With each repetition that worm got longer
Extending its reach into my very core
Supplanting whatever had been there before

My Tennyson, Shakespeare, Donne and Blake
Were all crowded out, make no mistake
By Horton, Maisie, Thing One and Thing Two
Cindy Lou Who, and Bartholomew.

Now when I sit down to write a poem
The Thing that comes out is an alien gnome
A green eggs and ham hash of nursery verse
What will become of me now that this curse

Has made me its victim, one hundred percent?
But I'm not upset, that's not what I meant,
That worm is a germ of incurable ways,
A lovable virus from those happy days.

Dr. Seuss was a wizard, of that there's no doubt
I can't really try to pull the worm out
Any more than I would try to extract
Those childhoods within me, still intact;

So infected I am, and infected I'll stay
Hoarding those stories until the day
When grandkids clamor for tales that are clever—
It's simply that I have been Seussed—forever!

TOUCHING UP THE GRAY

I am aging
like cracked vinyl waiting room upholstery
        in Clairol's *Clove* brown.

Like a gray heron balanced
on one knobbly leg, scanning the marsh
        in bamboo socks

imprinted with cats. Aging faster
than a speeding silver bullet
        to Lois Lane's
        telltale temples;

loving dye as Carson's
        balding scalp
loved the furred animal of illusion.

Aging not as Art knows itself
untouchable, but as soft-shelled crab's
        translucent calculus

knows it must harden. Traveling Einstein's
        light time machine
        as dopplered train blares, fades;

in the mirror two distant particles
birth ∞ death, spooky discourse
        across deep dyed dark,

looping tails join cruel script:
        Nature's eternal
        ampersand.

Sparse-breasted robin
        on winter wings,
I dye to season
        whitening skies.

WAKE-UP CALL

In that splice where night meets day
light nudges heavy and resisting dark,
and I lie teasing the edge of a dream,
deciding nothing,
a single bird finds the seam
in the seamless round of time and motion,
tears it with a bugle call
as clarion as an angel's
and as certain.

As morning breaks to clamor
of birds, cars, trucks, mowers,
I lie clinging to my soft roost
deciding how best to breast this day,
thinking how hard-hearted was that bird
to rise and pluck from torpid night
the first ripe seed, fresh worm of light
and with one brave heraldic blast
summon us to the feast.

WHY I LIKE TO PLANT POTATOES

It's not just for the eat—
the cooked fresh-in-skin
moist cream sweet, the butter
sharpened with salt—
but also for the labor,
the square-nosed spade's
splintered wood handle,
how it slices the dense
layer cake of earth,

sweat, backache, thirst,
foot-deep trench, seed chunks
bedded sprout side up,
Red Nordland, Yukon Gold
buried six inches
in spring's wet warmth;
for each round surprise,
tight skin, firm flesh
cool in the palm.

For I am not a thin-armed girl
gathering bits
left in spent fields
while the combine of war
rakes through long years,
who collects soiled shards
so carefully in her apron;
I live fatly, plant
for the rich grit of earth
in my fingernails;

as my cat pirouettes
to snag her plush toy
in midair,
I plant to pleasure
a tuber buried
deep in brain's stem
that swells with
the untried rubric
of survival.

I COME TO HEAR THE MOJAVE POET, NATALIE DIAZ

*On April 23, 1859, clan chiefs came as ordered to hear (Lt.
Colonel William) Hoffman's terms of peace. Hoffman gave
them the choice of submission or extermination. (Wikipedia)*

She calls herself *part* Mojave, but it's the part that inherits the
    salt taste
of drowning, stands before a white-capped sea, warrior destiny
    manifest:

blood wounds bind her words, rattle the liver,
lodge like bleached bone in her gall. Hearing,

I am vulture fed on massacre, plucking eye of buffalo.
She is fresh meat and gristle and I swallow whole

morsels made tough on desert grass, blasted by white wind.
Tell me. Let me visit ancient pride, trials

of reservation hunger, belly empty of more than food,
see a desert river homeland blanched, sanded raw.

Let me follow this trail beaten with alcohol, drugs, life
dulled as commodity; feel how living prejudice still scarifies.

Let me feel dry parchment pulled through veins,
remains of a people of dreams and visions—

surely she would be called *sumach a'hot,* gifted—

not least in a cunning tongue that licks words to acts
of love, unspools barbed wire-torn family, clan;

how she aims a phoenix-feathered lance, red flint-tipped
at whitewashed walls; hurls it hard enough to stick the point.

AFTER THE BALL

Clipped grass, dirt blown
on bronze raised name,
implacable numbers:
Dad would be 94 today
had he rounded those last
months his last year
of not really being here,
mind, flesh fused
to nursing home sleigh, horses
hitched, snow charged to fall.

Graveside, memory's voice:
    After the Ball was o-ver
    Maggie took out her glass eye—
    silly song to make his grave
    child laugh.
    Stood her false leg in the cor-ner,
    mischief in his tuneful voice,
    Hung up her wig to dry—
    there were more lyrics,
    but by now the girl
    would give in, giggle.

I flap at dead grass with moist tissue.
Mom cries, glances at blank space
reserved for her name.

    By the last lines the girl was play
    angry because Dad was laughing
    and she was smiling, in spite of herself.
    Oh, you should have seen Mag-gie—
    as if the girl knew she would be
    Maggie some day, having fooled

the world, but coming home
to all that emptiness,
Af-ter the Ball.

CONSIDER THE BEDBUG

Flat brown oval
          six-legged freckle
skilled surgeon
          painless puncture
vascular tanker
          fills up at the pump
bloats on buffet
          between the sheets
bloody meat
          all you can eat
waddles home
          to seam or crack
curtains drawn
          in the secret dark
safe and unseen
          in the secret dark
to belch blood,
          mate, procreate
to never be seen
          in the light
hitchhike the world
          follow its need
to feed again
          while the great world sleeps
it's all they know
          or can ever know
or would maybe ever

  choose to know
and they are happy
          and they are legion.

INTRUSION

I surprise the dock:
my sodden step
fletched with shadow.

Below, one great blue heron
startles.
Unfolds, flaps,
turns water to air.

A second slaps:
flustered splash to whish of flight.

Slow, grand lift, long necks retract,
legs, slender shafts, like memories trail,

two yellow beaks
like arrows of light.

LATE

Always, one old man has dallied too long,
intermission over, everyone seated, house dark,
players on stage, and pissed off by
this speeding up of time,
grudgingly navigates the aisle, feeling his way

through broken glass, hot coals, a minefield,
toward the empty seat in row three.

It's hard to watch his pained progress,
hard not to imagine
the rush of fast cars and foxholes,
bride, threshold, taut thighs and buttocks,
always late home, dinner cold, child in bed,
carelessly consuming the rich commodity
that now consumes him.

There, row three, in the seat next to his empty one
a woman's white head faces the living stage,
too absorbed now to worry
whether he is wending his way
or lying on the men's room floor,
never to be late again;

see how she leans forward,
lips parted to her own pleasure,
catching each line of this last act;
how she fails to notice him arrive, turn, align,
find the armrests, bend and surrender to gravity,
then nudge her arm with his elbow,
wanting to know what he's missed.

REPLY TO JENNIFER

Mail to: jenbabs@icu.edu
From: hilbmar@icu.edu

Ms. Babson:

You and I have not met, yet I am undoubtedly known to you as a Professor of English Language and Literature at this university and the wife of your Archaeology professor and thesis advisor, Dr. Charles Martin. In turn, your e-mail message to my husband, which you signed Love, Jennifer, tells me all I need to know about you.

Last night, my husband asked me to check his e-mail to discover which of his graduate students had expressed interest in the New Mexico dig during the January winterim. You see, outside of the archaeology lab, Dr. Martin is the archetype of the absent-minded professor. He relies on me to handle the clerical aspects of his position and to keep after such mundane matters as seeing he eats a healthy diet and wears matching socks. In return he gives me his complete loyalty and devotion—a symbiotic cooperation that has served us well for the past 26 years, a stretch of time longer than you have been alive.

There were six e-mail messages, including yours. As you know, there are only three slots open on the team for this very promising archaeological expedition. This means that three of you will be disappointed; but more on that later.

By the way, none of the other messages closed with "Love." Sincerely, Yours truly, Your student, and two Thank yous, but not one other "Love."

The other five students, while they may have the greatest admiration and even affection for my husband, evidently understand that to bestow this endearment upon him remains the sole privilege of his wife, daughters, and other close family members. I have no reason to believe that you are any less astute, or that some carelessness in your upbringing might have led you to regard "Love, Jennifer," as a proper closing for a student addressing a professor of any gender.

I am keenly aware of the effect of Dr. Martin's tousled, just-out-of-bed good looks, the nearsighted squint and weathered brow that have lent a rugged masculinity to his formerly soft-boiled aspect.   Over the years he has been the object of several student crushes, both female and male. I fear that you, Ms. Babson, must now be numbered among that misguided group.

Still, I think it unlikely that you are a true voluptuary, given your current field of study.   Fondling moldy skeletal remains, scratching over a square foot of desert for hours at a time—what could be more stultifying? It has always taken my most devoted ministrations to raise my husband from the dead, so to speak, after a long day at some dig.

No, I suspect you are rather more like a kitten that contemplates a majestic tree. The tree is irresistible to her: the freedom of it, the stretching of her young muscles, the heights she may attain! Rashly she climbs, and suddenly finds herself out on a limb in a very precarious position indeed. Does she jump into the void, without a snowball's chance in hell of achieving flight? No, Ms. Babson, the kitten is a sensible animal. She knows her limitations. After yowling for a while in self-pity, she swallows her pride and backs down the tree.

Not all that long ago, I was a young graduate student like you, and I remember well the temptation to see sexual adventuring as a means to success. After all, you ask yourself, why not seduce that older, distinguished professor who holds the keys to your academic future in his hands? Why not allow those hands access to your undeniable physical gifts, and with that one clever stroke catapult yourself into a position of feminine power?

I am confident that you will not be that foolish, Ms. Babson. Be guided by the feline model and think very carefully before you put yourself at risk.   What can you possibly hope to gain? A brief fling with a man old enough to be your father who, once the packaging is gone, is revealed to be well past the sell-by date? A man whose vigilant wife knows without being told that he has ordered egg salad for lunch instead of the prescribed tuna? A man incapable of artifice or subterfuge, who wears his heart, as well as his lunch, on his sleeve?

I often wish that some older and wiser person had advised me of the dangers of such youthful passions. Joseph Conrad writes that youth is "the deceitful feeling that lures us on to perils, to love, to vain effort—to death." I hope you may take this warning to heart and apply your talents, whatever they may be, to the pursuit of higher goals than the seduction of a happily married man.

It is time, my dear, to back down the tree.

As I am a true ally in your quest to become a person worthy of mature love and respect, dear Jennifer, I therefore inform you that you are not one of the three students selected for the New Mexico dig. The customary interview I hold with each candidate will not be necessary in your case. I am sure you will initially feel somewhat aggrieved by this decision, but to quote Hamlet, "I must be cruel only to be kind."

Do not think to ask Dr. Martin for redress in this. He gives me absolute authority in these matters. Devoted as he is to the contemplation of the extant remains of persons long dead, Charles finds the complicated affairs of the living to be a nuisance more happily avoided. Perhaps if you are still around next year—

Now I must end. My husband arrives home momentarily and will be looking for his supper.

Yours *in loco parentis*,

Dr. Hilary Bellingham Martin

_____

Institutional excellence / Caring faculty / Unlimited potential—Reveal yourself at I.C.U.!

ANGEL OF MERCY

It is mid-July in this ungodly summer of 1863, and we are still at war with the secessionist south. Coming into the kitchen from the back garden, I hear Maman in the front parlor, talking with a man. My heart jumps on the slim chance that a mistake has been made and the male voice might be Papa, or Charlie. I put down my basket of young summer greens and rush to the parlor; but no, the man is a stranger, another wounded soldier, seated in a wheeled chair, his left leg amputated just above the knee. I sigh. I thought we were done with caring for the wounded. This one at least looks to be well on the road to recovery.

"Mirabelle, dear, this is Mr. Parker. He will be our guest until he is strong enough to travel back to his home in—where was it, Mr. Parker?"

"Virginia, Ma'am. The Union part, of course." While the bulk of Virginia joined the Confederacy, the western shoulder of the state remained faithful to the Union.

"Naturally," Maman replies, always gracious. The French "Maman" sounds much the same as the American "Mama," but I realize now that this is one of the small ways in which my mother can revisit the French heritage she left behind when she married my American-born father.

I guess that Mr. Parker is not much older than my 20 years. He has curly brown hair, a strong brow, sturdy shoulders and arms. But his face is pale, with the sunken look they all had from damage that goes much deeper than the physical body.

"Mr. Parker, may I present my daughter, Mirabelle Ross."

"A great pleasure, Miss Ross. Miles Sutton Parker, at your service." He smiles ruefully and glances down at his empty pant leg. "That is, if a cripple can indeed be of service to anyone."

"Now, Mr. Parker," Maman scolds gently, "a brave soldier like you -- I am confident that you will enjoy a long life of service to all and sundry."

I add, rather too sharply, "yes, you should count your blessings. You are lucky to be alive." I do not mean to be uncharitable, but men and boys have died in my arms, and my own father and brother will never come home again.

Mr. Parker looks at me intently, bows his head slightly. "Please forgive me, dear ladies. I am as humbled by your wisdom as I am grateful for your care."

Now I know how this one cheated death: he could charm his way out of anything.

* * *

It is two weeks since the battle that raged for three days and nights around Gettysburg. Here in our once thriving town, businesses were shut or used for makeshift hospitals. Everything that could be spared was given to sustain the troops that had come to our defense, some from as far north as Maine. As they came into town we women ran out with loaves of bread, cups of water, salted meat. Some younger girls flirted, giggled, their heads turned by the sight of so many handsome young soldiers. I already knew enough to be sobered by the spectacles of this war. While Maman and I gave out the clothes and shoes that once belonged to my brother and father, it was all I could do to hold back tears and smile at these men who were likely marching to meet their deaths, as Papa and Charlie had, in a place far from home.

In those dark nights during and after the battle, as the women of Gettysburg sat tearing old muslin into strips for bandages, there were stories about families that had been divided by geography, brother forced to fight brother, even father against son. This was unimaginable to me. The women whispered how many of the Confederate dead were left to rot where they fell on field, hill, or stream. Although I hate the rebels with all my heart, this, too, was something I could hardly credit as the work of civilized men.

*   *   *

With Mr. Parker settled comfortably for the night, Maman helps me prepare for bed, unpinning my hair and brushing out my long auburn curls. "My beautiful daughter," she says softly, "this war has been hard on you. You should be in Philadelphia now, dancing with nice young men at parties."

What she means is, finding a husband. I was 18 years old when this infernal War Between the States started at Fort Sumter. I had a few suitors, not one with a worthwhile thought in his head. Having just turned 20 this May, in Maman's eyes I must begin my search or risk becoming an old-maid, But if I ever marry, it will be to a man with noble thoughts and the courage to speak them.

"Hush, Maman. You know I'm not one for parties and foolishness. Any young man worth his salt will be out fighting, not wasting his time at parties. I'd much rather be here with you." Soon after the news came about Papa and Charles, I secured a position as a tutor at the Young Ladies Seminary where I had been educated. I earn only a fraction of Papa's former income at the bank, but it keeps us from starvation. At the Seminary I teach the girls to read and do their sums, but also to think and learn about events and places outside Gettysburg. I feel most strongly that women should not rely only on men for their knowledge of the world.

Maman puts down the brush and strokes my hair with her hand. I have always loved it when she does this. She sighs and says, "Mr. Parker is from Virginia. Perhaps he knows Fredericksburg."

I flinch at the name of the place where my father and brother were killed, almost eight months ago, in the noble and just cause of preserving the Union.

"The one thing I could possibly wish for in this life would be to find where Papa and Charles are -- buried." Maman turns to leave, but I grasp her hand. We cling to each other in the flickering light of the tallow candle, each of us sobbing softly. We are alone in the world now, except for a sprinkling of relations in France. I must do my best to take care of my dear mother, and protect her from any more pain.

*   *   *

The next afternoon Mr. Parker dozes in the summer sunshine in our kitchen garden, where he ate his lunch. He stirs at my approach, and a book slides from his lap to the ground. We both know he cannot reach it from the height of his wheeled chair. I pick it up and a piece of paper slips out, a letter, written in a woman's hand. He carefully tucks it back between the pages.

"The letter is another memento of war, Miss Ross. My fiancée regretfully informs me that she is unable to bear my -- reduced prospects." His laugh is wistful, but without bitterness.

"Oh. I am sorry, Mr. Parker." His former fiancée must be hard-hearted indeed to reject a man who fought so bravely in the Union cause.

"Well, perhaps some things happen for the best. On reflection, I do not believe Clarissa would have been content as a farmer's wife."

A farmer? That would explain his well-muscled shoulders and arms, the callused hands. Remarkably well-spoken, though, for a farmer.

"And so, Miss Ross, are you an only child, like me?"

I stiffen. "I had a brother. He and my father died at Fredericksburg."

His brown eyes find mine. He sighs deeply. "In my home state. I regret your loss more than you can possibly know."

I nod to acknowledge this strange remark, pick up the lunch tray and turn to leave.

"Miss Ross, please. If I may detain you a moment longer, there is something I must tell you, though the consequences may be grave indeed."

Alarmed, I put down the tray and sit on the garden bench. "Why, Mr. Parker, whatever is the matter? Are you in pain?"

"Yes, in pain, but not as you may think. I am sick at heart. This damnable war. Miss Ross, in truth, I am not a Union soldier. I was with the 24th Virginia infantry when I was wounded."

Shock and horror catapult me to my feet. "A rebel!"

"Yes."

This man is the enemy. I must run away, shout for help, sound the alarm!

"Please, if I may be permitted to tell you my story."

I am so unprepared for the sudden anguish in his voice that I find myself seated again, if only on the very edge of the garden bench.

"Thank you. You see, I was born and raised on our farm, River Oaks, two hundred acres in a beautiful Virginia valley."

Two hundred acres! So he is not a farmer but landed gentry, a rich southern slave owner who never did an honest day's work in his life! My revulsion renewed, I stand to leave, but Mr. Parker seems to take no notice.

"My Father,' he continues, "was always stubbornly against slavery. Our farm hands and domestic help were manumitted men and women, paid a living wage. This arrangement was not popular with our slave-holding neighbors. We had long been ostracized, but as the secessionist fever spread, we were branded as abolitionists. Mysterious fires and other mishaps beset us. We lost livestock and crops. The situation became intolerable to my parents, so they moved to a small homestead in western Virginia."

Mr. Parker stares ahead, his gaze fixed on some distant point in memory. I sit down again, warily, yet too curious now to leave.

"I did not want to risk losing our family claim to the land. Against Father's wishes, I stayed on at River Oaks. Of course our Confederate armies made liberal use of my house, livestock, and crops, but allowed me to stay and work the farm. Until last month, when the 24th Virginia arrived on its way north. These were fighting men from the mountains, rough and unschooled but fiercely determined. They gave me a choice: march with them, or be shot as a traitor."

Mr. Parker shifts uncomfortably in his chair. Sweat beads his brow and his face is flushed. He may in fact be a clever, scheming liar, and I resolve not to be taken in.

"I went with them, praying all the while for the war to conclude before I was forced to engage in battle. You may imagine my distress, Miss Ross, at the thought that these troops might do some injury to my parents, who, begging your pardon, were now Yankees! I marched north with them, crossing the Potomac until we reached Chambersburg, where we encamped on the enforced hospitality of the residents of that fair town."

As much to admit he is a thief and plunderer; but his account rings with a strange truth and gives me pause.

"After two days, the troops began an eastward march. My division, under command of a Major-General Pickett, remained as rear guard in Chambersburg. On July the first we had word that a battle had begun outside Gettysburg. While the men in our brigade chafed to march east and join the fight, I secretly prayed that the battle would be concluded before we were called up to engage it. As you may surmise, my prayer was not answered. The order came and at 2 a.m. the morning of July second, we marched the long dusty miles eastward to Gettysburg."

He licks his parched lips. He is clearly uncomfortable in the hot summer sun, but I will not move one muscle to fetch this rebel some water, or to move him into the shade.

"Shortly after noon, we were deployed in an open field beneath the ridge where the Union soldiers were positioned behind a low stone wall. I thought our situation unwise, since there was little cover in the field. It was an afternoon much like today, the sun beating down on us with wearying force. Then our artillery began a fierce bombardment of the Union lines, which the enemy answered with a rain of iron from their batteries above us on the hill. By some luck or divine providence, Miss Ross, I survived this hellish bombardment with only superficial wounds. In the silence that fell when the artillery fire finally ceased, all that was heard were cries and pleadings from those who had not been so lucky."

These horrors are true. I recall too vividly hearing that below Seminary Ridge, the waters of Marsh Creek ran red with blood.

"But there was no time to assist the wounded, since in the next moment none other than Pickett himself came riding through our ranks. 'Up, men, to your posts,' he cried. 'Don't forget that you are from old Virginia!' Here I must admit a shameful truth, Miss Ross. Upon seeing the courage of my fellows as they rose to the fight, I was spurred by pride and loyalty to join the charge. I now put it down to a kind of mental derangement. In any case, I ran with the others toward the enemy position, through a curtain of dense smoke, trying not to trample on the men who had fallen before me, when suddenly I stumbled over that stone wall to stand face to face with a soldier in blue. It is impossible to describe the confusion, the deafening sound of musketry at close range, the clash of bayonets, and always the unending shouts and cries battering my ears."

Mr. Parker wipes his brow with a trembling hand. He seems unable to continue. I can see how much he suffers, yet I do not know how to react. I feel angry, confused. "You need not distress yourself further, Mr. Parker. I do not care to hear more."

Again, something wild and desperate in his look prevents me from leaving.

"Please, indulge me a moment longer. This man in blue, whether young or old I cannot say, or of what size or stature. All I saw clearly was the barrel of his musket pointed at me, the crack, the flash of fire, and then a blaze of pain that cut my leg like a hot knife. I pulled the trigger of my rifle, and then -- blackness.

I was found behind Union lines. I had no uniform and might have belonged to either side. My only identification was a letter addressed to my parents in western Virginia. When I regained consciousness and realized they had taken me for a Union soldier, I did not correct the error."

I sit, amazed. If what he says is true he is a coward, as I assume all rebels to be.

And yet -- "Why have you told me this, Mr. Parker? You could as easily have kept silent."

He blinks against the hot July sun and looks down, unable to meet my eyes.

"This War of the Rebellion is a fool's errand for the South, Miss Ross. My beloved Virginia lies desolate and ravaged, and for what—the right to hold other human beings as chattel? A bitter waste, in an unjust cause."

He coughs, swipes at his perspiring brow with his handkerchief. I want to hate him. He is Johnny Reb himself, spinning a web of honeyed words. What if he is a spy, planning to use me to gain information? It is my solemn duty to turn him in! But I am somehow unable to move from this bench.

"I may have killed that man, a man who was probably someone's father, or brother. You have lost both, Miss Ross. If you can find it in your heart to forgive me, then I think I may begin to forgive myself. Whether you decide to turn me in or not is of little importance."

I am stunned. His account has taken everything I thought I knew about honor and duty, and turned it upside down. Tears sting my eyes. "Some wounds never heal, Mr. Parker. You must look to God for your forgiveness."

I wheel around and run inside. I will not burden Maman with the weight of Mr. Parker's secret, nor will I act until I have had time to think over what he has said. A landed southerner with no slaves, who refuses to answer the Confederate battle cry? I avoid Mr. Parker for the remainder of the evening and retire early, but spend the night thinking about him, tossing and turning in my bed with my mind pulled one way, my heart another, never suspecting the shock waiting for me in the morning.

* * *

I crash through the hospital doors. "Doctor, please come quickly. Our patient has taken a bad turn!"

The room is crowded with cots and chairs bearing bandaged and broken men, the last of the soldiers wounded in battle. Dr. Welkin is inspecting a man's foot, scowling over a blackened bandage.

"Now Mirabelle, as you see I am busy."

"Maman took in his breakfast this morning, and he was feverish. But he was fine yesterday." Fine, I thought, until I condemned him with my hard words. Now it is I who am guilty and in need of forgiveness.

The doctor lets out a long sigh. "Even with a good clean amputation there's always a chance of sepsis." He gives some instructions to the nurse, washes quickly, and comes along with me.

As we enter the parlor, Mr. Parker is sitting in his chair, cheeks flushed and eyes bright, yet chatting with Maman as if in the peak of good health.

"Dear Dr. Welkin, it was good of you to come so quickly." Maman rushes over to him and offers her hand. "Our patient looked feverish while he slept, so I sent for you immediately. But Mr. Parker assures me he is not ill."

Dr. Welkin frowns. "Yes, well, *hmph*. Might as well have a look at him, long as I'm here."

"And of course you will take some refreshment. It's the least I can do to make up for having troubled you."

My mother's musical voice has a softening effect on the grumpy bachelor. "Not at all, dear lady. Always a pleasure--" he mutters, then wheels Mr. Parker into the next room while Maman and I go to the kitchen to prepare the tea.

"Do you think Mr. Parker is really all right, Maman?" I try not to let the guilt sound in my voice.

"I felt sure of it as soon as I spoke to him, but it was too late to call you back." She measures out the tea leaves and an equal portion of dried chicory. Since the war began, tea has been very scarce and frightfully expensive. "With all that's happened my nerves are quite frayed, and I jumped to a hasty conclusion. I do hope poor Dr. Welkin will forgive me."

I have to smile at this. Maman is the only one who cannot see how much the good doctor admires her. He can never take Papa's place, but it pleases me to know that Maman has a good and devoted friend to count on.

We bring out the tea tray, such as it is, with no jam for the bread, and no sugar or cream to mollify the bite of the brew. As the men return to the parlor, I begin to pour.

The doctor settles into the armchair. "I am satisfied that the stump is clean and dry, with no sign of sepsis."

I feel a surge of relief, and at the same time the word stump catches in my heart. The loss of a limb must be agonizing. Mr. Parker is a victim of this terrible war, almost as much as poor Papa or Charlie. I was a fool to believe that a man's worth may be judged by the uniform he wears, or his readiness to kill others. I will not turn him in.

Dr. Welkin continues speaking to Maman. "Our patient has a mild case of heatstroke. He should take the sun for shorter periods until he is accustomed to the out of doors again."

So that's it. Too much sun, yesterday in the garden!

Mr. Parker looks at me and smiles. "It was quite scorching in the garden yesterday."

All my uncertainty gone, I smile back at him. "I feel sure it will be milder from now on."

"I'll leave a name and address of a prosthetics maker, young man. You should be ready to travel in another week's time," Dr. Welkin says brusquely, then becomes as placid as a lamb as Maman escorts him to the door.

Alone now with Mr. Parker, I fight a sudden shyness. "I believe you to be an honorable man, Mr. Parker. If my forgiveness still has any importance to you, I give it freely."

He searches my face with his warm brown eyes. I blush.

"I believe you to be an angel of mercy, Miss Ross, sent to me by Heaven. How can I repay your kindness?"

"Since you ask, Mr. Parker, I will speak my mind. Maman and I wish to go to Fredericksburg, to find where Papa and Charlie have been laid to rest. But I fear travel may be difficult for some time, and dangerous for two women traveling alone."

He answers my boldness with a nod. "Say no more, Miss Ross. It would be my great honor to serve as escort. After I learn to manage with my new limb, we will travel to my parent's house and when it is safe, from there to Fredericksburg. You and your mother have our hospitality for as long as you wish."

Who would have thought it? Kindness *and* courage, in a rebel. "Then, we have a bargain?"

He extends his callused hand. "You have my pledge, Miss Ross."

I place my hand in his, pleased to accept something so noble as a pledge. For in these times of distrust and hate, this does not feel like a bargain. It feels for all the world like the beginning of healing.

Peter E. Murphy

LABOR DAY: ATLANTIC CITY

This is the last you'll see of Philadelphia drivers
who make illegal U-turns on Pacific Avenue,
then park themselves on the sand that will grit
against their skin as they Humvee the traffic-jammed
expressway back to the city that spawned them.
This is the day when Showboat and Trump
and the second tallest building in New Jersey
that reveled on the Boardwalk for just two years,
fold five thousand dealers into the street.
Also losing his job is Mr. Peanut because he swung
his cane at the juvies who tried to trip him.
Everyone wants to sell their houses.
When they advertise themselves,
the casinos euphemize *gambling* as *gaming*
and are required to state, *Bet with your head. Not over it.*
There are other words you need to know—Shoobie,
Ar-Kansas, Lucy, Wawa, FEMA—to make sense
of this island. My friend Sandy lost too much in a storm
named after her. Born on 9/11 long before the fall,
she dreams of waves, not jetliners, crashing into buildings.
What else can you say about a woman who backs up against
    history?
There are 228 steps to the top of the lighthouse
where you can see how the tide rips away at the dunes.
They put up a cage so you can't throw yourself off after
    climbing.

John Petrolino III

BIG APPLE TIME

1)
We laid on my
bed on a lazy afternoon
covers smoothed over
the tight bed clothes
and I held her loosely
in my arms.
the simple way
I'd run my hand through her hair
and gently grace her
arm with the back
of my hand...
gazing into her eyes
the clock said it was
time to go...
then it said it was
time to rush
we laid there
a few moments more

2)
in the car I pressed
the accelerator pedal down
far and made my way
into the express lane.
when the road was
open and straight, I'd
reach over and touch
her hand or leg.
feeling her skin and
the heat from bodice.

on the Turnpike,
marshes and buildings and
rail cars zoomed by
and we shot over a
bridge to a stand still
before looping through
the Holland tunnel.

3)
on Bleeker street we
held hands pacing the
walk, bounding in and out
of stores.
Slowly stirring sweetener
into coffee and leisurely
sipping away.
I'd stare into her
eyes and see cars in
my periphery go by,
taxis off loading passengers
and take off for another fare.
standing on the corner of
Cornelia we
waited from my friend...
nearly an hour late.
I didn't worry as I
wrapped my arms around
her from behind.
I could not fault my friend.
At his hotel room,
fresh white sheets
were probably below him
as he gazed into
a woman's eyes.

Robert Pinsky

AT PLEASURE BAY

In the willows along the river at Pleasure Bay
A catbird singing, never the same phrase twice.
Here under the pines a little off the road
In 1927 the Chief of Police
And Mrs. W. killed themselves together,
Sitting in a roadster. Ancient unshaken pilings
And underwater chunks of still-mortared brick
In shapes like bits of puzzle strew the bottom
Where the landing was for Price's Hotel and Theater.
And here's where boats blew two blasts for the keeper
To shunt the iron swing-bridge. He leaned on the gears
Like a skipper in the hut that housed the works
And the bridge moaned and turned on its middle pier
To let them through. In the middle of the summer
Two or three cars might wait for the iron trusswork
Winching aside, with maybe a child to notice
A name on the stern in black-and-gold on white,
Sandpiper, Patsy Ann, Do Not Disturb,
The Idler. If a boat was running whiskey,
The bridge clanged shut behind it as it passed
And opened up again for the Coast Guard cutter
Slowly as a sundial, and always jammed halfway.
The roadbed whole, but opened like a switch,
The river pulling and coursing between the piers.
Never the same phrase twice, the catbird filling
The humid August evening near the inlet
With borrowed music that he melds and changes.
Dragonflies and sandflies, frogs in the rushes, two bodies
Not moving in the open car among the pines,
A sliver of story. The tenor at Price's Hotel,
In clown costume, unfurls the sorrow gathered

In ruffles at his throat and cuffs, high quavers
That hold like splashes of light on the dark water,
The aria's closing phrases, changed and fading.
And after a gap of quiet, cheers and applause
Audible in the houses across the river,
Some in the audience weeping as if they had melted
Inside the music. Never the same. In Berlin
The daughter of an English lord, in love
With Adolf Hitler, whom she has met. She is taking
Possession of the apartment of a couple,
Elderly well-off Jews. They survive the war
To settle here in the Bay, the old lady
Teaches piano, but the whole world swivels
And gapes at their feet as the girl and a high-up Nazi
Examine the furniture, the glass, the pictures,
The elegant story that was theirs and now
Is a part of hers. A few months later the English
Enter the war and she shoots herself in a park,
An addled, upper-class girl, her life that passes
Into the lives of others or into a place.
The taking of lives—the Chief and Mrs. W.
Took theirs to stay together, as local ghosts.
Last flurries of kisses, the revolver's barrel,
Shivers of a story that a child might hear
And half remember, voices in the rushes,
A singing in the willows. From across the river,
Faint quavers of music, the same phrase twice and again,
Ranging and building. Over the high new bridge
The flashing of traffic homeward from the racetrack,
With one boat chugging under the arches, outward
Unnoticed through Pleasure Bay to the open sea.
Here's where the people stood to watch the theater
Burn on the water. All that night the fireboats
Kept playing their spouts of water into the blaze.
In the morning, smoking pilasters and beams.
Black smell of char for weeks, the ruin already

Soaking back into the river. After you die
You hover near the ceiling above your body
And watch the mourners awhile. A few days more
You float above the heads of the ones you knew
And watch them through a twilight. As it grows darker
You wander off and find your way to the river
And wade across. On the other side, night air,
Willows, the smell of the river, and a mass
Of sleeping bodies all along the bank,
A kind of singing from among the rushes
Calling you further forward in the dark.
You lie down and embrace one body, the limbs
Heavy with sleep reach eagerly up around you
And you make love until your soul brims up
And burns free out of you and shifts and spills
Down over into that other body, and you
Forget the life you had and begin again
On the same crossing—maybe as a child who passes
Through the same place. But never the same way twice.
Here in the daylight, the catbird in the willows,
The new café, with a terrace and a landing,
Frogs in the cattails where the swing-bridge was—
Here's where you might have slipped across the water
When you were only a presence, at Pleasure Bay.

Derek Pollard

FAST THE FORGE

Tonight the moon

Just full

Our names, waking

To measure, water

Let out o'er March grass

                              Raising

    Seed

Caterpillar

                              First

              To cinch

                          Which clasp, what

              Turning

Death once, near

Morning

Death once

The slipped embrace

Susanna Rich

HURRY UP, SUNRISE: OCEAN GROVE

Alligator profiles scud the horizon—
    gray cirrus shearing gray cirrus.

        Still, as if our scrub, scrub of this earth
could create undiffracted dawns,

the beach Zamboni rakes up Dunkin' Donut cups,
    scrambled fishing line, shards of plastic

        lighters and barrettes; swirls around sleeping-
bagged lovers; combs the sand with long wendings

of musical staffs with blue mussel notes.
    I rose early enough, and it's time, the almanac says—

        but there's no sun—the blood yolk ooze of it,
the butterscotch burn that says *I am here.*

        I slice the air with my walking,
backwards, sometimes, in case the bright tongue flicks,

just then, into flame.
    Yet, clouds crowd exactly where the sun might rise,

        as I Bic words onto a Pinot Noir wine label I found,
like a Chinese cookie fortune on the beach—

I write *led by the gulls* above its bar code,
    scratch *battleship, pier with flag* over its Government Warnings,

        as if something I write might
     conjure the sun from those soft-toothed maws,

those gold-rimmed pelts.
     As if *because* I was looking the sky would

          turn to sudden lace and I might have what I have:
     my toes noodled into wet morning sand,

my secular hands pressed in prayer,
     over my parting lips.

Bob Rosenbloom

ADOPTION PAPERS

When our parents
were away, my older
brothers teased me.

They said I was adopted,
that the papers were up
in the kitchen cabinet

with other important
papers we kept beneath
the portable broiler,

which I couldn't reach.
When I asked them to
take the papers down,

they said a judge had
ordered them moved.
If I'm ever recognized

for something important,
I'll deny I'm related
to those morons.

Christine Salvatore

LEAVING TOWN

I try to ignore those fathers
and mothers, the ones who taught
that steel beams are better than
the soft tips of grass, foundations
cannot be made of soil and root,
that stability is all.

But three years in a city can take
the wildness out of you. Words
become concrete, thoughts like
cracked sidewalks. You always know
where you are going, when to walk,
when not to. This is a place
with appointments and time budgets,
where early morning is a time to get going
instead of talk. Last night
in a bar on Delancey Street
your breath collapsed on me.

I'll tell you, there is still that urge
to fight over quarters at the pool table,
stay till closing, walk home
on a less than brightly lit street.
I can't help noticing
how your sigh fell from me
onto water-marked wood that had long
forgotten the falling of leaves, the thrill
of a storm wind. My mind rises high
above the squareness of buildings,
the blackness of asphalt, tries
desperately to leave this vacancy
and take you with me.

S. O. Schiro

After graduating from Alfred University, S. O. Schiro began a career in residential remodeling while pursuing interests in music, painting, and writing.

In 2000, after attending a poetry reading, he joined a writing group and began writing poetry and prose on a regular basis.

HOBO

I joined a poetry group
Like a dirty limerick
Slipped into their anthology
I nod and smile
And steal thoughts
I have no opinions
No advice.
A black sheep
In the literate flock
I remember as a child
I wanted to be a hobo

DESIRE

You slid through my soul
Like a snake on silk
Helpless,
I grabbed you
And hung on
        When I was young
        I never said love
        When you admit to your dream
        Its over
        Had I trusted my senses
        My heart may have found a home
        And freed me
        To hunt for stones and feathers
You look through me with unfocused eyes
You move your hands across my skin
Warm me
Entwine me, surround me,
Melt me,

Dissolve me. . .
>What?
>Yes.
>Yes, of course I think you're pretty.

INSTITUTION

Locked away
Alone in this holding pattern crowd
Purgatory bus station of rare departures
And fluorescent lights
Shouted words without thoughts
Ruined children with headphones
Marching back and forth
Telling each other they're going somewhere
Saving up the months
As if they were worth something
A downpayment on a future

All lined up in no direction
Trash talkin' attention deficit boys
Acne and methadone, stuck-in-neutral boys
Laugh a little too loud boys
Turn your life around boys
Less-than-zero, gave up long ago boys
And just-don't-know boys

A warehouse of bad judgement, bad luck, and bad intentions
Afraid of what they've seen, and what they haven't
Thinking about people they knew in a better time
Treading water
Crying in the dark
When the bad time catches up to them
And won't let go

RESTLESS

Soap me up and slide all over me
Gimme a smoke and a black coffee
I'm on daylightwastin' time today
Life in the waiting room took a wrong turn
And I'm sixteen years old for a while

Soap me up and slide all over me
I'm a boy and a man, and we're both restless
Dress me in lycra and a cowboy hat
Run with me
We'll chase the day like kittens on coke
Frantic foolish fun for a while

Soap me up and slide all over me
While the coffee's hot
We'll trade another day for one good hour
We'll take a little time out from forever
So soap me up and slide

SNOW

The little boy inside of me
Roots for the snowfall
To pile up
And shut down the world

To reduce the infinite

To bring it down to my level

To turn this scary, ugly place
Into a white amusement park

SWM

You just walk into my dreams
Like some disturbing but magnificent commercial

And I wonder what you wonder
When the lights are out
And the moon shines through your window

Do you think about
Those moments of perfection
Pressed against each other
In sweat and peace

I put an ad in the personals today
Single white male
Seeks anyone

TURTLE

A snapping turtle beneath the swallows
You see the world as a swamp
From the prison you call yourself
Closer to the snakes
Than the eagles
Safe in your shell
Feeding on the young and the weak
Stealing their futures

"That's the way the world is," you say
As you eye with scorn
The ones that got away

Life has cheated you
Made you a reptile
So you cheer when the hawk makes a kill
And rejoice in the weakness of others
And profit from the helpless and fragile

How could they possibly deserve
What you will never feel

Friendless
But never lacking allies
You may even share a carcass
From your Cayman Island account

TWO

There were two of us
And I was one of them
We came together
In times
Before calculation

We were friends
And one day
I just said
"Come home with me"
Or maybe,
No, most surely
We both said it

Occasionally,
I surprise myself
And do the right thing
Like I said,
Instinct

MEN ARE PIGS

Drums up
Now kettle drums
Louder, primitive, visceral
And. . . cymbals
Orgasm

Phase out drums
Strings up
And pan back
Window, river
Sky, clouds
Strings fade
Lose focus
Beautiful,
And cut

Tracy had slept with artists before
Thinking somehow
They would be better lovers
But Lance was her first film student
She lay there wondering
About her judgement
"I've got to be more discriminating"
She thought

She rolled her head
On the pillow
Hoping to find
Someone familiar
Lance was staring at the ceiling
Lost in post-production visions

As she got up to shower
She looked back to those eyes
Those eyes that had seduced her
They were beautiful eyes
But they didn't see her
She wondered if she would even make the credits

ALIM

Alim was one of three stallions
In a herd of thirty Arabians.
We had been transported to seventeen hundred acres
In the middle of nowhere, New Mexico
By a new age cowgirl with old money
She was Paris Hilton, Joni Mitchell,
Annie Oakley, and Leona Helmsley
All in one

Every morning
We would lead the horses out to pasture.
Alim would greet me
Craning his neck over the gate
For me to attach his leadshank
"Hey buddy, why the long face?"
Alim didn't see the humor in my greeting
I thought it was so funny
I said it every day

Alim had a more physical sense of humor
He would stick his face in mine
For me to stroke his neck
And scratch him behind the ear
Like a dog

And just when I began thinking
He really loves this
He would suddenly take a big bite
Out of my shoulder
And attempt to drag me over the fence
By my shirt
Ideally, ripping the sleeve off
While rearing backwards
To avoid a certain slap in the nose

As we walked out to pasture
I would make disparaging remarks
About his bloodline
And the fact that the other two stallions on the ranch
Were more expensive than he was

But nothing I would say would bother him
As long as he had a piece of my shirt
Hanging from his mouth

IN SPACE

In space
There is no sound
There is no yelling
No commercial messages
No crying
You can't fart
And your knees don't creak

In space
Taxes are low
And you don't need vitamins

There are no ground rules
And there is no home team

In space
Because of all the stars
Diamonds are no big deal
There is mass
But no weight
Don't ask me to explain that

In space
You don't have to move over
No one is obnoxious
And they're on the metric system

In space
Water doesn't know what the fuck to do
There are no emotions
And there is no camouflage either

In space
There is no prostitution
Relationships are based on gravity
No one is on top

In space
When you rob somebody
You can't get away
There is no away

In space
Deaf mutes play tricks on the rest of us
And mimes exhibit an air of superiority

REMEMBER

We were there, when it opened
The presidential library
In Texas
We were there
Behind the barriers
Behind the police
Behind the cameras
Cameras with blinders

Many of the dead and disabled couldn't make it
But one could see, that many had
Veterans and Iraqis, side by side
With gold star mothers

The dismembered, the discarded, the disillusioned
Showed up for the show
Whistle blowers and high school hippies
Historians, media, clergy,
And three members of congress

Estimates say
That fifteen to twenty million of us
Congregated that day
Behind the barriers
Behind the police
Behind the cameras
The cameras with blinders.
They would do their job
Just as we had

It was an impressive crowd
But it was far too late
For anything good to happen

REBECCA

A large translucent woman made of jello
Was in my dream this morning
As my tongue slid slowly between her lips
Her body, both solid and liquid, moved with mine
Not in a frenzy of pleasure
But like waves meeting each other on still water

Now I'm no fool
I know a dream when I see one
And though the universe is said to be infinite
How many raspberry jello women could there be?

I called Stephen Hawking
If anyone knew, it was this guy

I asked my question and waited
Apparently, he types the answer
With his nose, or something
Finally, the answer came
In that distinctive voice of his
"NOT MORE THAN SIX OR SEVEN"

LITTLE SILVER

What would you want with a sand box
When you have the earth
I still smell it, the earth
All disrupted and pushed aside
And I still smell the lumber, the pine
Waiting to be the house I would live in

New houses, fifties America
For all the new people

I'd hike up Church Street
Past Lovett's nursery
Past the post office,
A little wood frame building
With a porch worn down over the years

No porches on the new houses
The new people didn't have time to sit around

Across the street, the big white church
And the cemetery, with its mysterious brick wall
A fortress guarding history

I remember the crude wooden bridge
Over the brook that ran through the school yard
Later, they would put that brook
In a big long cement pipe

I remember the wild strawberries
In the field at the end of Church Street
And Sickle's corn
Piled high on a picnic table by Rumson Road

I remember walking up town to the Sugar Bar with a quarter
To get my dad a pack of "Luckies"
The two pennies change, right there in the wrapper
My commission on a twenty-three cent sale

For adventure, we would follow the brook
From Sickle's pond, all the way to the river
Through the woods
Through the swamp
Jump the brook
Don't sink in the mud
Be home before dark

POKER NIGHT

Every once in a while, the poker game would end up at our
    house
A small, middle-aged convention of fifties America
Looking back, I understand these guys, and their poker night
    attitude

I knew them a little bit, the big smiles and handshakes
They greeted me as a man, their gift to one who has no idea
They lived through the depression, they lived through World
    War II
No surprise, they saw me as some cute, clueless little nestling
I felt this canyon between us
We were certainly from two different worlds
These were no peers of mine

I shook hands real hard, and looked them in the eye
"Hiya Ernie, how's the missus?"
I liked these poker guys.
What I actually liked was the setting
The little vacation from real life
No jobs, no families, no competition
But the game on the table
The money was real,
Just enough to make the night interesting
But not so much as to remind the players
Of the real gambles, the real consequences to face
Tomorrow morning, every morning

I watched all the poker guys
I watched them play
In a cloud of cigarette smoke and laughter
I watched them play
This is where I want to be when I grow up
This is where they wanted to be

TED

So, this guy next door, Ted
Whenever I would see him, out in his yard
He would always have something to say
I would make some pointless comment about a shrub
And Ted's response would always contain some insight
Into the nature of the human condition
Apparently, Ted considered himself
Both a historian and an anthropologist

I like the way the rhododendrons remain a deep green
Throughout the winter

The Mexicans are taking over the Colored's neighborhoods

If you water in the evening, you'll need much less water

Arabs don't have homosexuals, you know why?

I feed my tomato plants once a month.
The soil isn't very good here

Everybody thinks the Jews control the media
But that's just what they want you to think
Because guess what

One day I called him 'encyclopedic'
A slight hesitation, and then he lit up
Like he was just nominated for a Nobel prize

Did you know Cameron Diaz was a lesbian?
Donald Trump is nothing like he's portrayed on TV
Ben Afleck is actually a Marxist, that's why he hates America

I couldn't figure out how anyone could gain
Such massive insight from watching TV
Maybe there's some special cable package
That only certain people are aware of
Ted does emit a kind of New World Order vibe
I mean, how else would he know the location
Of the Ark of the Covenant

No, he didn't tell me
But I could see he wanted to

C. John Schoonejongen

C. John Schoonejongen is a born-and-raised New Jerseyan who has lived in, hiked in and slept in nearly every corner of the state. A professional writer and editor who worked in the state's newspapers for more than 30 years, John wrote a well-regarded state politics column from 2011 to 2014. For his poetry, he draws upon his summers at the Jersey Shore, his hikes in the Pine Barrens and his train rides to Newark and New York City. He resides in Millstone Township with his wife and two children.

A MILLION STREAKS OF LIGHT

He sat and told me of his life
In pieces, great and small—
Where he is, bearing no trace at all of where he was.
I see myself through a prism, he said,
A million streaks of light,
Not whole, never whole.
I'm spoiling for a fight
With those who stole my story and threw it to a brutal wind;
My "I am" spread among the stars at night.

DEAD SEA TURTLE

So much was seen
By the dead sea turtle
Before waves hurled him upon the sand
And gawkers gathered
To capture a glimpse of he who had been free.

ELIZABETH

I pass her daily,
See the grime on her bosom,
Wish to wipe it clean
And offer her my embrace.
Tired, useless gesture
For weary Elizabeth.
In the spent city
Arms are not needed for love,
But ceaseless lifting.

FOR LEONARD

I've listened to you and wanted to sing
And dwell on my consonants
Like bees in a hillside vineyard
Spreading life on a late-summer day.
I've read your words and wanted to sing
In a small room where those who know
Snap and nod with a got-it gravity
And murmurs of acceptance and assent.
I have always wanted to sing,
Always wanted to hear my own words
Pouring like water across cracked rocks,
Rushing into caves and echoing, echoing.
But I was afraid to open my mouth
For fear that water was not wine,
That echo was laughter,
That the awkward drip in the quiet after the flood
Was the music of a soft, myopic fool.

LITTLE MORNING

He sees the sun's rising
Before the golden light arrives,
The patter of his tiny feet, my trumpet call.
His gentle breath, the hurricane that shakes the castle walls.

Sleep is a feeble boundary for a honeyed smile.
And in these shadows, dim and celebratory,
Nothing is routine, and everyone's a hero.

Wake, wake, says the whisperer, and laugh with me
Before the world whisks you away.

Take the silver and the wood
And let us run upon the sand, hand in hand,
On this, our only day.

OLD MAN AND THE MUSE

I once knew a man who was a poet.

He was older and lived inside himself. While his family, children and grandchildren, buzzed around him, he sat in a chair near the doorway and wrote. I think he may have spoken 10 words to me in the three years I knew him, but during that time he must have written hundreds of poems, his inner thoughts and feelings expressed on paper without lines.

He was not Yeats, Eliot, Neruda or Stevens. He could claim no grand insight or brilliant innovation. But he wrote nonetheless. I tried to ask him once why he wrote, but he could give me no coherent answer.

He was not the kind of man you would think of as a writer. He was not well read. He had little interest in the arts or even the world outside his home. He was a strong man, with hands that could crush yours. He was a salesman and then a security guard after retirement. He fathered six children by two women. His daughter was my girlfriend.

I had a glimpse of what it was that caused him to retreat into a world of verse and meter. His was not an easy life. One of his grandchildren (the daughter of a son from his first marriage) was kidnapped and brutally murdered. His second wife was a terrible woman, feared by her family for her violent and vitriolic outbursts. Not a day went by when she didn't insult or belittle someone. He was estranged from his two older children in part because of her viciousness. And while she was making her own children feel worthless, he sat in his chair writing. Perhaps he never cared. Perhaps he was defeated. I like to think it was the latter, because his love for his children was in his written words. Sadly, those words never crossed his lips.

I'm sure he's passed on by now. But I always hoped that he continued to write even after his wife died, for I know he loved her even though she hated him. She was his tormenter and his muse.

And what of his reams of poetry? What of those words he so carefully put together, night after night, while the rest of his family watched television, played games and tried to avoid the wrath of an unstable woman? What of his life beyond the flesh and blood and bone? Some of his verse may have been spread among his children, but a couple of them would have had no appreciation for it. My old girlfriend, I think, would have valued some of the work. Maybe her own children read his words from time to time. I have no doubt that a lot of it was discarded, turned to compost.

Many of us write for our legacy. In books and libraries, on microfilm and in cyberspace, my writing is sprinkled. I have laid low the mighty and inspired the faithful. But in the end, my work is ephemeral, connected more to institutions rather than me personally. Like an old man writing in a corner while the world around him turns, I am anonymous to all but a few. And, still, I write.

One Saturday, my wife and I attended a festival at Rutgers University. One of the areas they had set up was for writing seminars and workshops. As we passed by, a young woman saw us looking at the billboard and shouted, "Vote for your favorite writer here."

"He's my favorite writer," my wife responded, pointing at me.

Of course, I was proud, but I couldn't help but feel that the girl laughed as we left. "Everyone's a writer," I imagined her saying and then shaking her head at the foolishness of our age and ignorance.

As my wife and I made our way around the campus, I saw the dreams and ambition of youth and wondered if there was room in a new world for an older man, still finding a voice. I wondered if I might yet bring the world to me through my words. Or was I just another poet whose words will enter the ground with him?

And, in a quiet communion with my past acquaintance and brother in verse, I prayed that where another old man's work was buried a flower grew.

ON A SWING

It was, she thought, the perfect moment. The date had been sweet and understated. Dinner at an eclectic restaurant and a quick walk to a neighborhood jazz club, where the smoky sounds from an old man's saxophone left her in the mood to consider possibilities.

He seemed to be a good man, kind and generous. Their conversation was easy, almost to the point of familiarity. He was handsome, tall and quick with a smile. In a tough dating world where the losers seemed to outnumber the winners by a huge margin, there was little doubt that he was a winner. So when he leaned toward her, she was ready, and she tilted her head so his lips would have no trouble finding hers.

Then she laughed.

It wasn't intentional. He had done nothing funny or odd. It was his goatee that tickled her, and in her nervousness she pulled away.

"What's the matter?" he asked.

"Oh, nothing. Just your mustache," she said.

It was true. It was nothing. But it was also everything. And after a few more quick kisses just to see if a lost moment could be recaptured, she said her good-byes and shut her door.

Caroline walked slowly through her house and sighed. Her kitchen was dark, but she did not turn on the light. Instead, she walked gingerly up the stairs, counting them as she stepped. A soft bed light glowed as she entered her room, and she began undressing. She looked good tonight, she thought. Dark jeans, a silk blouse and a suede jacket—one by one were removed and laid carefully on a small chair. She caressed each item as if it had life and meaning.

Her 30s were being kind to her. While her friends chased children, she attended spin classes. Most people thought she was still 25, and in some ways she felt 25. Her deep green eyes, thin nose and pale, perfect skin made men and women alike look at her twice. Her dark hair, long and straight, was pulled back behind her ears. It hung in a perfect, straight line just below her shoulder blades.

She admired herself in a mirror, swinging her head from side to side. She felt her hair brush against the skin of her back and she shivered slightly before pulling on a T-shirt and shorts.

"He thought I was hot," she whispered to herself. "I know he did."

Caroline smiled and shrugged.

She knew she would not see him again. After all, the kiss had not been perfect. It was perfect she wanted. Caroline had it once, and there was no settling until she found it again.

She opened her bedroom window and breathed deep. It was a summer night, much like the night when, at 14, she sat on a swing at the playground by the lake and moved back and forth, the only sound the creaking of the chain. He was pushing her higher and higher, hands first on her shoulders, then as she soared above him, on her hips. His hands felt good, soft but strong. It seemed forbidden, the way he touched her, though she did not know why. All she knew was that her hair was blowing in her face and the breeze was cool on her arms.

Not a word was spoken. Caroline was afraid to break the spell. He was shy, she thought, even though he was a popular boy, a junior varsity second baseman who was bound to be the varsity starter next year. And he was beautiful—soft, playful eyes, blond hair and a smile that always made her lower her head and blush. She felt pretty when she was with him. That night, however, she felt more than pretty. She felt. . . she couldn't place how she felt, but it was different, confusing. She was sensitive, restless, anticipatory, almost electric. Swinging higher was the one thing that kept her senses from overwhelming her. So she flew, closer to the stars than to earth, she thought—the tiny lights dancing as the swing moved to and fro.

He pulled his hands away and let her swing by herself. She felt free, and she missed him at the same time, and that just made her body crave his touch even more. There was no feeling like this before. She almost felt like laughing, but her throat seemed swollen shut. No words, no sounds, just the movement of her legs beneath the swing.

Caroline sensed him still standing behind her and soon she began to rest, the rhythmic creak of the swing's chain slowing as she came back to earth. His hands touched her again, not pushing this time, but merely guiding. He cupped her shoulders as the swing slowed even more. Then his hands covered hers as she held the chain and the swing stopped.

He was directly behind her now, and she looked over her shoulder to see his face. There it was, that smile that made her blush. Those blue, blue eyes. Only this time, she did not lower her head. She kept looking at him, locking her eyes on his. He moved, she bit her lip and closed her eyes. She felt his breath (Caroline swore later she could hear their hearts beating). And they kissed. No long and passionate kiss. Just a second or two, maybe. When he pulled away, she opened her eyes and looked at him. He was still smiling. Then he pulled back on the chains and pushed her, high and away, on the swing. Higher and higher, she swung again, smiling while he touched her back.

That night ended the same as others. Her head on a pillow in her room. The window open. The curtains pulled back so the moonlight spilled on the floor beside her bed. But she could not sleep. The rush of air, his eyes, his touch and a slight and fleeting kiss that made Caroline feel for the first time as if the world was hers and the stars really were close enough to touch.

Yes, it was perfect. And it was not repeated. She tried. Boyfriends and lovers came and went. But none could measure up. Some came close, and she loved them. But perfect? No.

Not even this nice man, the latest who found her captivating and gorgeous, was enough to break the spell. She crawled into her bed and rested, thinking for a moment about tomorrow's work and the weekend ahead. The world was not standing still. Six a.m. was not far away, and she needed sleep.

The curtains waved and flapped as the wind blew through her bedroom window. The moon peeked through the clouds, as she began to drift away. She stirred and smiled, wishing she were a young girl again with the breeze in her hair, swinging free.

Lauren Schmidt

WHAT I LEARNED ABOUT MY FATHER ONE DAY AT THE BEACH IN 1986

When the last bit of string slipped off the cardboard spool and my kite
sailed into the sky, lifting further and further away with each gust
of after-thunderstorm wind, I collapsed into the sand and screamed.

My father ran off the beach, then rushed north on the Boulevard,
the strip alongside the boardwalk which blinked with arcade lights,
sent smells of sausage sandwiches and zeppoles through the air.

My mother tried to appease me by sharing my brothers' kites while,
for two miles, my father hunted mine, all the way to Point Pleasant,
    stuck
to a moving bumper. When he returned, red and breathless, cheeks
    and chest

flecked with mud kicked up by the treads of the car he chased, he gave
    me
my mangled kite. We knew it would never fly again, but we took turns
running it till dinner anyway, laughing every time it came hurtling
    down.

Jennifer E. Stahl

Jennifer E. Stahl is a middle school language arts teacher in New Jersey. She is also a poet and short story writer whose publications include *Edison Literary Review* and *This Broken Shore* (Coleridge Institute Press). Jenny's love of poetry started as a preteen when a copy of Emily Dickinson's collected poems showed up in her Easter basket. Her Chilean roots lead her to read Pablo Neruda, an episode that left her panting and sweaty in the poetry section of a Barnes & Noble in the late 80s - an episode that also secured her place as a sucker for a love poem. A self-proclaimed "slow poet," Jenny's writing routine usually starts with a few tears before she circles the wagons and puts pen to paper. She'd like to thank the Jersey Shore Poets for being an important part of her creative life.

When she's not writing lesson plans or taking drum lessons, Jenny likes to spend her time reading, going to the movies, and napping epically. She currently lives in Monmouth County with her boyfriend, writer Gregg Glory [Gregg G. Brown], and their adoring black cat, Miu Miu.

FALLING

Your naked shoulder—
I want to bite it.
See my squinting eye?

I will not allow myself to fall in love with you here. I roll over
    onto my side in your bed– it's always *your* bed, *your* empty
    fridge. I watch your chest rise and fall in the glow of the
    TV, tempted to slide my hand up under your T-shirt. You
    fell asleep so easily as I grappled with *Should I stay the
    night?*

I stare up at the ceiling, unsure and unsung. I poke my left
    foot out from under your comforter to get some relief
    from the oven heat baking our bodies. I crack one big toe,
    then the other. You sigh. I try to memorize your profile–
    your parted lips, your quiet ear.

I suddenly want to go home—so I can fall in love with you
    when I am alone, in my own bed.

I want to sink my teeth
into your skin
And then kiss the bruise.

LOVE POEM

> *Love is beautiful.*
> *Love is butterflies and needles.*
> *Love is hard. ~~5th grader*

I am a blanket thief.
In an alligator death roll
I'll strip you bare in bed—
But I promise I feel bad about it.

The couple dressed as clowns at the costume party
is having an argument.
She says too loudly, too drunk,
All you give me are scraps of joy.
He pulls off his red plastic nose.
You hog the comforter is all he says softly.
His squirting flower wilts.

Come—I'll be the big spoon tonight.
But I'll fling the blanket off you at 3 AM
and pull at your hospital corners.
I am the butterfly and the needle.

MORNING DRIVE

Monday morning's drive along the Navesink River
moves slow as October bees,
fat snowflakes chase the chilled wind—
wide as potato chips
white as teeth
flying odd and joyful

Tuesday morning
I drive along the Navesink
and think of you.
Do you forget me a little when I'm gone?
Do you steal my pillow
and run your hands up the river of my side of the bed,
trying to capture the heat I've left behind,
sheets rippling like wake?

Wednesday morning is full of birds
floating on the Navesink

heads bowed down in prayer.
Are they praying for an early spring?
I imagine their cold legs
dangling in the water like straws

Thursday morning I'm running late,
running cold
I race along the Oceanic Bridge—
the Navesink is mostly frozen,
white icy shards wedged tight
like mountain peaks
as if an earthquake happened only here
and pushed the river up and up and up

Friday morning's sun glare
shines on the Navesink
like a necklace I want to wear.
I want to walk across the floe
and not share it

Saturday morning before sun-up
I dream of the Navesink tribe.
I see turtle totems
flying over the river, soaring
claiming the land,
the cliffs and creeks.
They invite me to stay
I tell them I can't fly
I tell them I can't swim

Sunday morning you make coffee.
What did you dream about?
I dreamed of the rolling hillside by the Navesink.
I dreamed of great oval pools of snow
caught in dips and vales, like milk for cats
I dreamed of water and ice and light

OBSERVATIONS ON DEAD THINGS

a dead shark ended up on a subway car in New York City
it was riding the subway to Queens, blood shining on its wet mouth
    like lipgloss
authorities threw it away at the end of the line

a dead thing lies in the sand in the front yard
hairless, grey like old milk
flies have started to use its body as an incubator
a bee chews—sucks?—at a small hole in the dead thing's face
deathly kisses

shoo—I wave my hand like a wand
the insects do not stop their work
they abuse the dead thing
filling its mouth with eggs, yellow filings
I use a newspaper to scoop up the tiny body
and throw the whole microbiome into the garbage can at the
    side of the house

children will rip the wings off Japanese beetles that hide in the
    rose bushes
just to watch them buzz in vain on the sidewalk

THE WAY THINGS SHOULD HAVE BEEN

I should have gone out in a blaze of glory,
    a crazy shrieking shrew unable to fathom the break-up
I should have cut off the sleeves from all his Armani suits
        tied his hundred Brooks Brothers ties into a hundred knots
        put Hello Kitty stickers all over the windshield of his Audi

called his boss and told her that every time he called in
    sick, he was lying

I should have peed in his Gatorade

I should have burned up his law school diploma in the furnace
        of that shitty townhouse we rented, the one with the blue
        zebra-print shag carpet
I should have subscribed his work email address to hard-core
        porn websites
        flirted with his best friends, all of them
        coughed on his cell phone when I had pneumonia
        dipped his workout clothes in gasoline

I should have known earlier that it was time to leave.

DOWN THE RABBIT-HOLE WITH SHARON BALLER

Epigraph
    *Alice started to her feet, for it flashed across her mind
that she had never before seen a rabbit with either a waistcoat-
pocket, or a watch to take out of it, and burning with curiosity,
she ran across the field after it, and fortunately was just in
time to see it pop down a large rabbit-hole under the hedge.*
                    ~~From Alice's Adventures in Wonderland

Elementary school librarians, like Sharon Baller,
know things, they hold secrets.
If you make friends with her
she will open worlds to you that you never knew existed.
She is Narnia.
She is Hogwarts.
She *is* Wonderland.

If I were ever to find myself down a rabbit-hole,
I'd want Sharon Baller with me.
She'd know exactly where to go
and she'd know the way home when it was time.

She'd lead me to the Great Mouse King's castle
and once there, the Great Mouse King would insist
that Sharon sit next to him and tell him stories as he
ran his spindly mouse fingers through her curly red head.

She'd be able to direct me to the Mole sisters' house,
Rose and Turnip, in case I wanted to buy
turnips from Rose and roses from Turnip.
And lifting her nose to the air she'd sniff, "Ahhhh."

She'd know which flower petals taste sweet (carnation)
and which did not (chrysanthemum, but they add zip to your
        vinegar, she'd be sure to tell me).
She'd know the moon's middle name (Pearl)
and a tornado's favorite card game (52 Pick-Up).

She'd apologize for making me late to the funeral,
and when I'd ask, "Who died?"
she'd giggle, then sigh and say,
"There's always a funeral for someone down the rabbit-hole."
And when we'd arrive at the fresh grave,
she'd pull an avocado from her pocket to lay in the mounded
        black dirt.

We'd sit together on a bench, Sharon and me,
and she'd tell me she'd been to Watership Down
and how the rabbits still played on the rolling green hills and
she'd reveal that she almost named her son Hazel.
I'd tell her my mother almost named me Clover and
we'd snort and laugh so spiritedly only chewing gently
on dandelion stems would stop us.

On the way home, she'd know which trees
liked to be hugged good-bye (weeping willows, of course)
and which trees would suffice
with just a handshake (the stoic oak).

If I were ever to find myself down a rabbit-hole,
I'd want Sharon Baller with me.
She'd know exactly where to go
and she'd know the way home when it was time.

BED

I.
Why don't I ever dream of you?
I push away the extra blankets
and gasp for breath
the pink tulips sit quietly on the desk,
mouths closed

II.
the sun shines on your sleeping face this morning
sweat gathers on your upper lip
I want to lick it away
taste your salt
sip you like medicine from a teaspoon
toss you into the saddle
and watch you ride away
waving your hat as I call your name

III.
Let's not make the bed today
leave the crumpled sheets—
the topography of sleep and sex

WHAT IS IT LIKE TO MAKE LOVE TO GWEN STEFANI?

What is it like to make love to Gwen Stefani?
Does she wear a ratty Rolling Stones t-shirt and her ex's boxers as
     pajamas?
Red-hot lingerie with lace and buckles and just enough satin?
Does she wear makeup to bed—red MAC lipstick in Ruby Woo
     that never rubs off onto the pillowcase?
Does she giggle when she slides under the clean bleached sheets at
     the hotel, holding her arms out, beckoning you to come closer?
Or does she turn her back to you so her strong, alabaster spine
     ripples like a fish swimming in milk?
Does she have moles and old scars and stretch marks? Probably not.
Does she roll like a pearl between your fingers, leaving behind
     iridescence on your wet thumbs?
When she arches her back, does her ceramic skin splinter
     into a spiderweb of tiny lines?
Does she need to be put back together again like Humpty Dumpty
     after the humping?
Is she too high maintenance? Just a china doll in lamb's clothing?
No doubt.

HEAD BOWED AT THE DRUM KIT

Our Father,
Who art in Heaven,
let me be a drummer.
I will fill the offering plate
with coins and golden hi-hats,
just let me be a drummer.
By Your Grace I will wrap my fingers
in white tape,
twirl a pencil in math class
like Tommy Lee,
join the marching band drum line,

a Salvation Army in red and gold uniforms
behind me.
Praise be the archangels
of rock and jazz and rimshot
whose hands beat and bongo
as they kick the bass drum hard.
Blessed be the downbeat when
Tré Cool
Jeremy Colson
and Ralph Peterson
pick up the sticks—
my metronome clicks to the swinging beat
of the thurible.
Christ! Make me a drummer.
All praise the riff, the lick, Sheila E
Bang a gong, get it on
I pray, make my paradiddles pulse
I will ride that cymbal to heaven.
O My God
Thy will be done,
make me a drummer.
Deliver me tempo and tom-toms and a solo.
Amen.

DOG DAYS

Let's have a summer to remember—
like people sometimes say. . .

Let's get tanned like new leather
travel the states
looking for the biggest ball of twine
complaining about the broken air conditioner
though you actually don't mind.

Let's stay in, instead—
let's be hermits—
we'll have a two-man book club
read Wolfe and Mailer and Didion
we'll spend days in our underwear
rolling around in literature,
the pages sticking to our sweat,
flies to fly paper, ants to the picnic.

Let's celebrate Christmas in July
and sing Bing Crosby tunes
to annoy the neighbors
What can they do?
It's a condo, so as long as they treat
the common area like it's their garage
we can sing Do You Hear What I Hear?
when the fireworks start.

Let's pick up ridiculous hobbies
like soap carving or drum lessons
and when the music teacher asks
What are your intentions?
let's laugh and not answer.

In the middle of the night
when we can't sleep
let's plan a family we never intend to have
give our children names like Benicio and Cricket
and tell them about the time we drove to the Gulf
drank margaritas and fly tails
salt sticking to our tongues as we laughed and kissed
smoked hand-rolled cigarettes as we watched the sun set
hot sand burning our soles
our souls half empty, half full.

WOMB

Epigraph
When the Sky God, An, had carried off the heavens,
And the Air God, Enlil, had carried off the earth,
When the Queen of the Great Below, Ereshkigal, was
given the underworld for her domain,
He set sail; the Father set sail...
~~Sumerian creation myth

My mother lies sprawled on the green tweedy couch in the living room of the trailer, eyes closed, she breathes long slow breaths. A box fan is set up beside her, pushing the hot July air over her sweaty neck, her rounded belly swollen with her growing August baby, her ankles fat with water retention. Strands of her long straight brown hair stick to her neck, her bare upper arms. She is not asleep; she is listening for my father's car to pull into the driveway. She hears some neighborhood trailer park urchins, squealing as they run through a sprinkler.

He pulls into the driveway and calls for her. Lorraine? I'm in the living room she says, eyes still closed against the heat. The afternoon sun has started to invade the room, one ray shining directly on my mother's face, tiny beads wetting her upper lip. My father looks at my mother, eyes soft as he thinks about his child growing inside her 19-year-old womb, the cradle of civilization. His own personal Mesopotamia. Let's go, he says.

They travel in his orange Chevelle with all the windows down. My mother has one leg propped up on the passenger-side door, her foot sticking out the window, red polish chipped because she can't bend that far anymore. Her long cover-up billows in front of her as the air rushes into the car. They don't talk, her eyes are closed again, her body is leaning across the bucket seat. My father gives her hand a squeeze, his own hand dirty with sweat and grit from working his shift at a gas station, his fingernails rimmed with motor oil that never washes off. He taps a thumb against her hand to the beat of Donovan singing on the radio. Jennifer, Juniper lives upon the hill. . . .

When they arrive at the beach, my father gets out to help haul my mother out of her seat. She stands next to the car, squinting as she looks toward the sea. She remembers coming here when they were 13, not yet knowing the love that was awaiting them. My father knows what she's thinking, he smiles at the memories of stolen kisses and of days spent on the beach from dawn until sunset. He walks ahead of her, picking a spot near the water, away from the day's last sunbathers. He drops to his knees and fishes around in the beach bag. He pulls out a garden trowel and starts digging into the scorched sand. My mother waddles over and stands above him, feet apart as if she were the beach warden. When he's finished, he stands and shakes out a beach towel, covering the basketball-sized hole. He helps my mother get comfortable on the towel as she positions her body and lowers her heavy, pregnant belly into the hole.

Years later, on a steamy August afternoon, while sharing the comfort of an oscillating fan, I will ask my mother what it was like being pregnant during the sultry months of summer and she'll tell me this story. I will see my father kneeling in the sand, bowing his head as if to the mother goddess Ninhursag. And I will know of being in my mother's womb, the earth relieving her burden.

WHERE THERE'S SMOKE

Remember the rules we all had as kids? *Change into your play clothes as soon as you get home from school.* Play clothes meaning last year's school clothes that were now too tight in the crotch and too high at the ankle for a whole day of school. *Don't eat two snacks in the afternoon or you'll spoil your dinner.* Really? Another granola bar could cause that much damage? *Be home each day by the time the streetlights come on.* More than once, I'd made it home by the first flicker of the streetlight illuminating my mother's face as she looked out the kitchen window to see me screech into the back yard on my blue bike with the white banana seat. I was a master at following rules. I enjoyed the attention I received for being a good girl. There were a lot of rules in our house, and we rarely ever questioned them or broke them. I think my mother kept the leash tight knowing her progeny came from a skilled, juvenile rule-breaker such as herself. And of all the rules, my mother's #1 rule was that we weren't allowed inside our friends' houses if their parents weren't home. My brother, Zachary, and I got used to asking, "Is your mom home?" when invited in to play Atari or Uno. We'd even take a step back as we asked, just in case Mom was lurking in the bushes, testing our resolve.

* * *

It was Saturday. Our neighbors across the street, two grungy little girls with dirty knees and oily scalps, were drawing with sidewalk chalk in their driveway. I envied their silky, black asphalt driveway, perfect for things like chalk drawings and roller-skating. Our own driveway was made of blue-grey stones, ones we certainly weren't allowed to play with.

My brother and I walked over.

"Why are you still in your pajamas?" Zachary asked. "It's almost lunchtime."

"Dunno," Tamara replied flatly, without looking up. The heels of her feety pajamas were worn through, and her skin was a rainbow of chalk dust.

I looked around at the colorful illustrations. The sisters were writing bad words on the driveway.

My brother asked, "What's a 'tit'?" as he turned his head this way and that, trying to read the giant scrawled letters.

"Come see what we wrote in the garage!" squealed the other sister, Marie. My brother trailed after her, entering the closed garage through a door at the back of the house. I suddenly thought, *Do garages count as 'in the house'?* I didn't know.

I watched Tamara. She was coloring a large block-letter 's' in the word 'piss'.

"Aren't you going to get in trouble?" I asked.

"No."

"Why not?" I shot back. I knew the girls' mother was permissive. They were often left alone at night and would pack their school lunches with candy and soda. But didn't bad words cross some sort of line in a mother's mind? I was suddenly annoyed that Tamara knew she wouldn't get into trouble for something for which I knew I'd get the belt.

"My mom's not going to see it," Tamara informed me.

I furrowed my brow. "You just wrote 'piss' in gigantic letters. How is she not going to see that?"

"Watch." Tamara walked over to the garden hose and turned on the spigot. She pointed the nozzle toward the driveway and began washing away all the words. In moments, 'tit', 'piss', 'hell' and 'booger ass' were nothing more than streaks of melting sherbet.

I was impressed. "That was smart."

"Yeah," she sighed, dropping the hose and walking toward the back of the house. I followed.

"Is my brother still in your garage?" I asked, anxious that I could not hear any voices. Tamara said nothing but kept walking toward the garage door. When she opened it, sunlight lit up the words 'turd car' written on the floor in green chalk.

I asked, "Are you going to wash that away, too?"

"Nope," she replied. "My mom always calls her car a turd because it's brown."

"Oh," I said, contemplating this logic. "Where's Zachary?"

"Inside," she said, jerking her thumb toward the open door leading from the garage into the house.

"Is your mom home?" I asked automatically.

"No, she's at work," Tamara said as she walked into the house.

Maybe I entered because I was worried about my brother. Maybe it was because I heard laughter. I'm not above blaming my neighbors because maybe they put a spell on me; I totally believe that could have played a part in all this. But my feet still crossed the threshold, and I boldly walked into a house without an adult in it.

We found Marie and Zachary sitting on the kitchen counter pumping Cheez Whiz onto a plate of crackers.

"This is delicious!" my brother chirped. He had Cheez Whiz on his lips and teeth. "Mom never buys this stuff for us!"

Tamara walked over and grabbed the can. She tilted her head back and pressed the nozzle. A three-inch line of electric-orange goo poured into her waiting mouth. My brother stared, fascinated and disgusted.

Marie shoved her sister and took the can. "Gimme it! I wanna try!" she shrieked. Marie stuck out her tongue and pumped a giant glob of cheese onto it. She started to laugh. The cheese fell out of her mouth and landed with a wet *plop* on the linoleum floor. She slid off the counter and walked toward the living room.

"Tam, let's show them our new game!" Marie hinted.

"Nah," Tamara muttered.

"Watch," Marie said, ignoring her sister. She walked over to the wood-burning stove. She reached up to a high shelf and pulled down a box of long-handled matches. She opened the glass front door of the stove, which, at first glance, appeared to be cool. Marie lowered the foot-long match into the belly of the stove and agitated the embers at the bottom, revealing a few burning bits. Flame immediately erupted at the tip of the match. Zachary said 'cool' as Marie pulled the match out and held it like a torch.

"What do you do with it?" he asked.

"We swirl them around in the air like sparklers," Marie explained. She demonstrated by making large circles with her arm, a cyclone of fire. She pretended to write her name in the air with her flaming pencil.

"I don't think we should be playing with these matches," I said, though I didn't sound convinced of this rule's use.

"My mom doesn't care," Tamara informed me as she lit one for herself.

In a flash the sisters started jabbing the matches in the air at each other in a mock sword fight. They lunged like they were a circus act.

Zachary picked up the box of matches; he briefly contemplated the picture of the cartoon devil on the box before pulling one out.

"Zachary, don't," I warned.

"It's just like sparklers!" he said to me as he gently tipped the match into the stove.

Sparklers. God, how I loved sparklers. I watched him wave the flame above his head in an arc. The match glowed and danced like he was a magician.

Meanwhile, Tamara and Marie had started marching through the house, moving their matches up and down like drum majors leading a parade. Zachary joined in and added "pa-rum-pa-pa-pum" to their music.

The performer in me wanted in, adult supervision be damned, so I lit a match and high-stepped through the house waving my flaming baton, my head held high.

At times we were too rough with the matches and chunks of ash fluttered to the floor, glowing embers that threatened to burn the house down. We stepped on them to make sure they were out. Soon, black streaks started to mark up the floors. I had a fleeting thought that we should use the garden hose to wash the smudges away.

In true kid fashion, our play quickly turned to chase. We ran through the house with the blazing scepters, in and out of rooms, as we squealed and slammed doors. We hunted each other, delighted to watch the flames elongate as we held the matches out like a sixth finger.

And then it happened, because, of course, it had to happen.

We were running one behind the other, a fiery conga line, down the hallway from the playroom to the kitchen. Once we got there, Tamara, the line leader, quickly turned around and bumped into her sister. Tamara's match touched Marie's chest. Marie shrieked. A sharp *tssst* sounded, and a wisp of smoke wound into the air above a small black hole in her pajamas.

I thought to myself, *We're going to die.*

The spell was broken. Zachary started to cry. Even Tamara and Marie knew a line had been crossed. I grabbed Zachary's hand, hauling him through the garage where I threw down our extinguished matchsticks. We ran blindly across the street because when you're running from the devil, you don't stop to look both ways.

My mother was getting the mail from the mailbox, and the moment we came streaking into the yard, she laid into us about the dangers of crossing the street unawares. *Did she not know we had come from inside our neighbors' house, the belly of the beast?* I stood there, traitorous tears pooling, hoping this was as far as the punishment would go, a tongue-lashing about traffic safety.

My mother stopped mid-sentence. "What's all over your face?" she asked, peering closely at my brother. I turned to him and saw he had black clouds of smeared ash on his cheeks and chin. Horrified, I raised my hands to my own face, hoping to wipe away any evidence of our near-death experience.

"And why do you smell like a campfire? What have you been doing?" she roared. Zachary started crying again. She looked to me.

A million excuses and lies tripped to the tip of my tongue. My knees buckled, and I hit the soft grass. I covered my eyes, and tears immediately gushed, making clean rivers through the spots of ash on my face.

My mother fell to the ground with me pleading, "What? What?" I choked out the story, revealing all details of our transgression. Zachary joined us on the ground and we hugged tightly, our mother grabbing to hold onto us, one watchful eye open.

BJ Ward

"AND ALL THE PEASANTS CHEERED FOR THE KING.
THE END."

I close the storybook and my son looks up.
He is swaddled with a bravery he knows nothing about:
    Astronauts floating across his pajamas—
    Soldiers bivouacking on his bookshelf—
    Knights on his lamp—so that his light
        shines right through armor.

"What's a peasant, Daddy?"
I don't think much of the answer: "A poor person."
"Like Grandma and Grandpa?"

And now the story is personal.

My son plays on the junkers my father works on forever—
the front yard is Grandpa's cold scriptoria
and he writes everything in blue collar serifs,
spending his days off rendering metal
into combustion.
Henry Ford invented the printing press
that churned out his Bible.

And my mother with her three shirts that fit—
her Bayonne accent a Cockney in my son's suburban world.

When I lend my parents money, that word has to be used—
lend— or else they wouldn't take it. Even poor people
have Pride as a lawyer.

I was his age when I first knew we were poor.
"Are we poor?" I had asked my mother.
Her eyes were just beginning
their descent deeper into her beauty—
they may have begun
to run away from the world just then,
at her older son's question—

"No," her mouth said, as obviously as possible.

Her hand stroked my hair.
It said, *I'm erasing that question.*

Her tremble said, *Yesterday my boss*
held an empty wallet to my head.

But were we rich somehow?
        C'mon—you know the clichés.
But were we rich in another way?

My father knows how to make stillness progress.
At the Foodtown, the cashiers always smiled,
for my mother was an S&H Green Stamp magnate.
My brother and I learned how to love
without dropping our eyes
below the neck.
If money's king, my family served it well.
We only asked to be able to sleep through the night.

And now, my own son is looking up at me,
seeing something he doesn't recognize.
I tell him, "Peasants live in kingdoms,"
and shut out the light—
The astronauts are still fastened in their flotation.
The soldiers still guard the fairytales.

Michael Waters

CAD

Whatever it was I'd done (or hadn't)
Almost a quarter-century ago,
Her rage erupted when we met by chance
In the coffee shop, each spilled invective
Raw in a room calm with Norah Jones' croon.

The uneasy baristas kept busy
While I scanned the sea of gaping laptops,
Its swift surge of hoisted heads, wondering
If her loathing had boiled up only when
She turned from dropping the crimped straw wrapper

Into the hole brimming with paper cups
To face the man with whom she'd spent one night
(Or less than one night) while her children slept
And her ex Ikea'd his guy condo
In sleek, taupe, post-adulterous closure.

We'd been tending each other's loneliness
However that evening had ended, but
Her snarled word was so 18th century
And ludicrous even as she lobbed it
That laughter broke her vindictive fever,

And we sipped our grande mocha frappés
Among the awake and amused voyeurs
Waiting to see if what had (or had not)
Taken place in the past might swirl around
To clasp us in prophetic happenstance.

Daniel Weeks

IN THE METHODIST CHURCHYARD, WEST LONG BRANCH

The hedge overgrown and
woven through with honeysuckle
vines and the grass
too high by half among the stones
lean hard against memory.

That man walking his dog
and talking too loud for heaven
on his cell breaks the hermit's
spell he came for. His dog
snoops for a quiet spot

to leave his load close to
the humped ground where
the once beloved Dr. Z.
N. Severn sedately lies.
Herr doctor, could you not

have saved yourself nor yet
this young boy, once much
grieved when these broken trees
were young? The tow-head boy
had closed his eyes, seeming so

like my son falling to sleep after
baseball and too many cartoons.
His kin came with august
trepidation to see his sweet head
laid against bleached satin—

young dryad in the hollow
of a tree. This was in the
last year of the Mexican War
and the parents, too, like
vessels heavy-laden, long ago

broke upon that self-same shore.
From the churchyard, that day
to this, the weathervane at
steepletop points always in
one direction. The man, barking

incoherently into his chatterbox,
his t-shirt covering an unsightliness,
and the dog, too, unmindful of
that ragged finger, seem even now
groomed to disappear.

Joe Weil

FOR CASSANDRA

Not having been heard
as if a waterfall, invisible, yet ever roaring
had fallen between her and the world;
and having been seen only in her coat of motley,
she moved as a crooked thing moves
scrabbling, scuttling, the whole of her day
spent tripping over the knottiest roots;
and when she died, when the waterfall ceased—
they heard her silence. This they filled
with their own voice—the common
tongue that licks the salt from prophets
until nothing is left but a stain.
She lived as one you might think harmlessly insane.
Catastrophe, she cried, Catastrophe—
while the sea kept up its lifting and falling mood.
Catastrophe—cries the soul—in solitude.

EARLY WINTER

From the half-rotten ash-tree's topmost twig,
a mottled cloud dives—and all the ash keys quiver,
while out a little further, a murmuration
rises, and falls upon the freezing river.
I join my own reflection to the geese
whose victory v moves from the rivers sedge
and skyward, a broken circle of rosary beads
vanishes. A blue jay takes the pledge
of his own name. Such a wild crested bird
must have a reason to the riot in his rhyme:

and then I see the red-tailed hawk that rides
on thermals, wings spread, how peacefully it glides
then drops—a thousand feet to snatch a hare
I bite my lip and bleed into its cry.

Daniel Zimmerman

WINGING IT

at the Raptor Trust refuge in the Great Swamp
a one-winged bald eagle big as a small man
scans my retina for its blind spot

doll-eyed owls wait for hollow bones to mend
& molt barred feathers illegal to possess
even if they fall from heaven on my head

& though my beard bristles like a porcupine
& though close enough to kiss you I'm half blind
I scan the far sky from the ledge I live on

doll-eyed myself but learning at last to hunt
from the great raptors' statuary action
one barred feather spiraling down from the sun

Visiting Writers' Biographies

James Arthur's poetry has appeared in *The New Yorker*, *Poetry*, *The American Poetry Review*, and *The New York Review of Books*. He has received the Amy Lowell Travelling Poetry Scholarship, a Hodder Fellowship, a Stegner Fellowship, a Discovery/*The Nation* Prize, and a Fulbright Scholarship to the Seamus Heaney Centre in Northern Ireland. His first book, *Charms Against Lightning*, was published in 2012 by Copper Canyon Press. He lives in Baltimore and teaches at Johns Hopkins University.

Renée Ashley is the author of six collections of poetry: *Salt* (Brittingham Prize in Poetry, University of Wisconsin Press), *The Various Reasons of Light*, *The Revisionist's Dream, Basic Heart* (X.J. Kennedy Prize in Poetry, Texas Review Press), *Because I Am the Shore I Want to Be the Sea* (Subito Book Prize), and *The View from the Body*. She has also published two chapbooks, *The Museum of Lost Wings* (Hill-Stead Poetry Prize) and *The Verbs of Desiring* (New American Press Chapbook Award) and a novel, *Someplace Like This*. She teaches in the low-residency MFA in Creative Writing at Fairleigh Dickinson University and does freelance editing; she's received fellowships from the New Jersey State Council on the Arts and the National Endowment for the Arts.

Emanuel di Pasquale was born in Ragusa, Sicily, in 1943, and came to America, by ship, in December of 1956. He went to Sleepy Hollow High School, in Tarrytown, New York, and graduated in three years. From 1966 to '68 he taught English at one of the original 'Negro Colleges,' Elizabeth State University in North Carolina. Then, later in '68 he moved to Middlesex County College, NJ, where he still teaches. He is the poet laureate of Long Branch, NJ.

Stephen Dunn is the author of 18 books of poetry, including DIFFERENT HOURS, winner of the Pulitzer Prize. Among his other awards are Fellowships from the Guggenheim and Rockefeller Foundations. W.W. Norton will publish his next book WHEREAS in February, 2017.

Melissa Febos is the author of the memoir, *Whip Smart* (St. Martin's Press), and the essay collection, *Abandon Me* (Bloomsbury). Her work appears in *Tin House, Prairie Schooner, Granta, The Kenyon Review, The New York Times, Glamour, Poets & Writers*, and elsewhere. The recipient of fellowships from The MacDowell Colony, VCCA, Vermont Studio Center, Lower Manhattan Cultural Council and others, she teaches at the Institute of American Indian Arts and Monmouth University and serves on the board of VIDA: Women in Literary Arts.

Frank Finale is the author of *To The Shore Once More, Volumes I, II,* and *III* which was published this year. He co-edited two poetry anthologies: *Under a Gull's Wing* and *The Poets of New Jersey* and was poetry editor (1996- 2012) for *the new renaissance.* www.frankfinale.com He is an essayist for Jersey Shore Publications magazines and guidebooks, www.jerseyshorevacation.com

Penny Harter's work has appeared in many journals and anthologies, and in twenty-two collections (including chapbooks). Her recent books and chapbooks include *The Resonance Around Us* (2013); *One Bowl*, a prizewinning e-chapbook of haibun (2012); *Recycling Starlight* (2010); *The Beastie Book*, an illustrated alphabestiary (2009); and *The Night Marsh* (2008).

She was a featured reader at both the first (1985) and the 2010 Geraldine R. Dodge Poetry Festival, and she has won three poetry fellowships from the New Jersey State Council on the Arts; the Mary Carolyn Davies Award from the Poetry Society of America; the first William O. Douglas Nature Writing Award for her work in the anthology *American Nature Writing 2002*; and two residencies (January 2011; March 2015) from Virginia Center for the Creative Arts.

    penhart.wordpress.com; www.2hweb.net/penhart.

Lois Marie Harrod's chapbooks *Nightmares of the Minor* (Five Oakes) and *And She Took the Heart* (Casa de Cinco Hermanas) appeared in 2016. Her 13th and 14th poetry collections, *Fragments from the Biography of Nemesis* (Cherry Grove Press) and the chapbook *How Marlene Mae Longs for Truth* (Dancing Girl Press) appeared in 2013. *The Only Is* won the 2012 Tennessee Chapbook Contest (*Poems & Plays*), and *Brief Term*, a collection of poems about teachers and teaching was published by Black Buzzard Press, 2011. She is widely published in literary journals and online ezines from *American Poetry Review* to *Zone 3*. See www.loismarieharrod.org.

John Hoppenthaler's books of poetry are *Lives of Water* (2003), *Anticipate the Coming Reservoir* (2008), and *Domestic Garden* (2015, winner of the Brockman-Cambell Award for the best volume of poetry published by a NC writer in 2015), all with Carnegie Mellon University Press. With Kazim Ali, he has co-edited a volume of essays and interviews on the poetry of Jean Valentine, *This-World Company* (U Michigan P, 2012). For *Connotation Press: An Online Artifact*, he edits "A Poetry Congeries." He is a Professor of Creative Writing and Literature at East Carolina University.

Charles H. Johnson is a Geraldine R. Dodge Foundation Poet in the Schools. He also is the poetry instructor for the Arts & Education Center in Middlesex and Monmouth counties, NJ, as well as a visiting poet for the Paterson, NJ, school district. He was a 2013 second-place winner of the Allen Ginsberg Poetry Awards for his poem

"Sunday Comics" and the 2011 County College Morris New Jersey Poets Prize winner for his poem "Leaving." His third collection "Smoke Signals" won a 2010 Paterson Poetry Prize for Literary Excellence for previous finalists of that contest. His chapbook "A Poet's Dozen" has been selected for e-book publication by Warthog Press. Web site: charleshjohnsonpoet.net

X. J. Kennedy has published ten collections of his verse, beginning with *Nude Descending a Staircase* in 1961. The latest will be *That Swing* in 2017. He has written a comic novel, *A Hoarse Half-human Cheer,* and twenty-two children's books. He has taught at Tufts, Wellesley, California (Irvine), Leeds, and other places. He's had recognitions including the Robert Frost medal of the Poetry Society of America and the Jackson Poetry Prize, given by Poets & Writers He and his wife and co-author Dorothy live in Lexington, Mass.

Adele Kenny, founding director of the Carriage House Poetry Series, and poetry editor of Tiferet Journal, is the author of twenty-three books (poetry & nonfiction). Her poems have been published worldwide and have appeared in books and anthologies from Crown, Tuttle, Shambhala, and McGraw-Hill. She is the recipient of various awards, including NJ State Arts Council poetry fellowships, a Merton Poetry of the Sacred Award, the 2012 International Book Award for Poetry, Kean University's Distinguished Alumni Award, and her book, *A Lightness, A Thirst, or Nothing at All* was a 2016 Paterson Prize finalist. Website: www.adelekenny.com.

Ted Kooser is a poet and essayist, a Presidential Professor of English at The University of Nebraska-Lincoln. He served as the U. S. Poet Laureate from 2004-2006, and his book Delights & Shadows won the 2005 Pulitzer Prize for poetry. His writing is known for its clarity, precision and accessibility. He worked for many years in the life insurance business, retiring in 1999 as a vice president. He and his wife,

Kathleen Rutledge, the retired editor of The Lincoln Journal Star, live on an acreage near the village of Garland, Nebraska. He has a son, Jeff, and a granddaughter, Margaret.

Diane Lockward is the editor of *The Crafty Poet II: A Portable Workshop* and the original *The Crafty Poet: A Portable Workshop*. She is the author of four poetry books, most recently *The Uneaten Carrots of Atonement*. Her poems have appeared in *Harvard Review, Southern Poetry Review, Prairie Schooner,* and elsewhere. Her work has also appeared on *Poetry Daily, Verse Daily,* and *The Writer's Almanac*. She is the founder and publisher of Terrapin Books.

H. A. Maxson is the author of 17 books—5 collections of poetry (*Turning the Wood, Walker in the Storm, The Curley Poems, Hook* and *Lemon Light*); a book-length poem (*The Walking Tour: Alexander Wilson in America*) and a novel in free verse (*Brother Wolf*); two novels (*The Younger* and *Comfort*—co-authored with Claudia H. Young); a study of Robert Frost's sonnets (*On the Sonnets of Robert Frost*), and seven works of historical fiction for young readers, co-authored with Claudia H. Young. Over 1000 poems, stories, reviews, essays and articles have appeared in periodicals, journals and anthologies. He has been nominated several times for Pushcart Prizes. He holds Ph.D. from the Center for Writers at the University of Southern Mississippi and has taught literature and creative writing for over four decades at the college level. Married to Maureen Maxson, a nurse and photographer, they are organic gardeners in Milford, DE.

Laura McCullough's manuscript *The Wild Night Dress* has been selected by Billy Collins as a winner of the Miller Williams Poetry Prize and will be published in February, 2017 by University of Arkansas Press. Her most recent books include *Jersey Mercy,* poems, Black Lawrence Press, and an edited anthology, *A Sense of Regard: Essays on Poetry and*

Race, University of Georgia press. Her other books of poetry include, *Rigger Death & Hoist Another* (BLP), *Panic* (winner of the Kinereth Genseler Award, Alice James Books), *Speech Acts* (BLP), *What Men Want* (XOXOX Press), and The Dancing Bear (Open Book Press). She edited *The Room and the World: Essays on the Poet Stephen Dunn,* University of Syracuse press. Her essays, memoirs, stories, and poetry have appeared widely in places such as Michigan Quarterly Review, The Southern Review, The Georgia Review, The American Poetry Review, Guernica, Pank, Gulf Coast, The Writer's Chronicle, Best American Poetry, and others. She has had fellowships or scholarships from Bread Loaf Writers Conference, Sewanee Writers Conference, the Nebraska Summer Writers Conference, the Virginia Center for the Arts, the Vermont Studio Center, Marble House, the NJ State Arts Council, among others. She teaches full time at Brookdale Community College in NJ and is on the faculty of the Sierra Nevada low-res MFA and has taught for Ramapo College and Stockton University. She teaches for the Stockton University Winter Poetry and Prose Getaway. She is the founding editor of *Mead: the Magazine of Literature and Libations.* Visit her at lauramccullough.org.

Donald "D.J." Moores, Ph.D., is a percussionist, author, and editor who serves as associate professor of Literature in the College of Letters & Sciences at National University in San Diego, California. He is the author of numerous scholarly articles and conference papers, as well as three critical books: *The Ecstatic Poetic Tradition* (2014), *The Dark Enlightenment* (2010), and *Mystical Discourse in Wordsworth and Whitman* (2006). In addition to compiling *Wild Poets of Ecstasy: An Anthology of Ecstatic Verse* (2011), he has also co-edited *The Eudaimonic Turn: Well-Being in Literary Studies* (2012) and, more recently, *On Human Flourishing: A Poetry Anthology* (2015). His teaching and research interests include (1) British, American and transatlantic Romanticism, (2) mystical/ecstatic poetry, (3) world literature, and (4) critical theory. An avid interdisciplinarian, he approaches these subjects holistically from a variety of critical perspectives.

Mihaela Moscaliuc is the author of *Immigrant Model* (University of Pittsburgh Press, 2015) and *Father Dirt* (Alice James Books, 2010), translator of Carmelia Leonte's *The Hiss of the Viper* (Carnegie Mellon University Press, 2015), and editor of a collection of critical essays on poet Gerald Stern (Trinity University Press, forthcoming 2016). She is assistant professor of English at Monmouth University and faculty in the Drew University MFA Program in Poetry and Poetry in Translation.

Peter E. Murphy is the author of *Stubborn Child*, a finalist for the 2006 Paterson Poetry Prize, *Challenges for the Delusional*, a book of writing prompts, and four poetry chapbooks. He lives in Ventnor and is the founder of Murphy Writing of Stockton University, which sponsors the annual Winter Poetry & Prose Getaway and other programs for poets, writers and teachers in the U.S. and abroad.

John J. Petrolino III is a Merchant Marine and writer. His work has been published online and print, notably: *The Idiom Magazine, Lips, The Edison Literary Review* and the first year English text book at Hampton University. His work was also featured in the World Spirt film *Greenwich Village* with David Amram. Petrolino has two books of poetry *Galleria* and *Congo Lights* and founded the River Read Reading Series in Red Bank, NJ. Visit him on the web at johnpetrolino.com.

Robert Pinsky's first two terms as United States Poet Laureate were marked by such visible dynamism, and such national enthusiasm in response, that the Library of Congress appointed him to an unprecedented third term.

Throughout his career, Pinsky has been dedicated to identifying and invigorating poetry's place in the world. Elegant and tough, vividly imaginative, Pinsky's poems have earned praise for their wild musical energy and range. Selected Poems (FSG, 2011) is his most recent poetry. His The Figured Wheel: New and Collected Poems 1966-1996 was a Pulitzer Prize finalist. Pinsky often performs his poems with eminent jazz musicians, in venues ranging from schools and universities to jazz clubs. His CDs PoemJazz and PoemJazz II House Hour, with Grammy-winning pianist Laurence Hobgood, were released by Circumstantial Productions.

Robert Pinsky is the only member of the American Academy of Arts and Letters to have appeared on "The Simpsons" and "The Colbert Report." For years a regular contributor to PBS's The NewsHour, he publishes frequently in magazines such as The New Yorker, The Atlantic Monthly, The Threepenny Review and The Best American Poetry anthologies. He is also the winner of the PEN/Voelcker Award, the William Carlos Williams Prize, the Lenore Marshall Prize, Italy's Premio Capri, the Korean Manhae Award and the Harold Washington Award from the City of Chicago. He teaches in the graduate writing program at Boston University. In 2015 Boston University named Robert Pinsky a William Fairfield Warren Distinguished Professor, which is the highest honor bestowed on senior faculty members actively involved in research, scholarship, and University civic life, and teaching.

Robert Pinsky's most recent book of poems is *At the Foundling Hospital*. As U.S. Poet Laureate, he founded the Favorite Poem Project, with the videos at www.favoritepoem.org and an annual July institute for K-12 educators.

Derek Pollard is co-author with Derek Henderson of the book *Inconsequentia* (BlazeVOX, 2010). His poems, creative non-fiction, translations, and reviews have appeared in *American Book Review, Colorado Review, Diagram III, Drunken Boat, E·ratio, Pleiades,* and *Six-Word Memoirs on Love & Heartbreak,* among numerous other anthologies and journals. Currently, he is Assistant Editor at *Interim: A Journal of Poetry & Poetics.* He previously served as Associate Editor at New Issues Poetry & Prose and as Assistant Editor at Barrow Street Press. He holds a PhD in English from the University of Nevada, Las Vegas, where he was a Beverly Rogers, Carol C. Harter Black Mountain Institute Fellow in Poetry and is now on faculty.

Susanna Rich. Poet, songwriter, and Emmy Award nominee, Susanna Rich is a Fulbright Scholar and principal performer at Wild Nights Productions, LLC. Her repertoire includes her poetry musical *Shakespeare's *itches: The Women Talk Back,* and *ashes, ashes: A Poet Responds to the Holocaust.* Susanna is the author of three poetry collections: *Surfing for Jesus, Television Daddy,* and *The Drive Home.* She received a Presidential Excellence Award for Distinguished Teaching at Kean University. Visit her at wildnightsproductions.com.

Bob Rosenbloom lives in Bound Brook, NJ with his wife and son. His daughter now lives in St. Paul, MN. Bob's a Certified Civil Trial Lawyer in NJ. His poetry has appeared in the Paterson Literary Review, Edison Literary Review, LIPS, US 1 Worksheets, among other journals. He runs a monthly poetry reading at the Bridgewater Public Library.

Christine E. Salvatore received her MFA from The University of New Orleans. She currently teaches literature and creative writing at Stockton University, in the MFA Program at Rosemont College, and at a public high school in

South Jersey. She is a Geraldine R. Dodge Poet and a regular faculty member for Murphy Writing Seminars. Her poetry has recently appeared or will appear in *Diode, The Longleaf Pine, The Fem, The Literary Review, The Cortland Review, Mead Journal,* as well as others.

Lauren Marie Schmidt is the author of three collections of poetry: *Two Black Eyes and a Patch of Hair Missing; The Voodoo Doll Parade,* selected for the *Main Street Rag* Author's Choice Chapbook Series; and *Psalms of The Dining Room,* a sequence of poems about her volunteer experience at a soup kitchen in Eugene, Oregon. Her work has appeared in journals such as *North American Review, Alaska Quarterly Review, Rattle, Nimrod, Painted Bride Quarterly, PANK, New York Quarterly, Bellevue Literary Review, The Progressive,* and others. Her awards include the So to Speak Poetry Prize, the Neil Postman Prize for Metaphor, The Janet B. McCabe Prize for Poetry, and the *Bellevue Literary Review's* Vilcek Prize for Poetry. Schmidt's fourth collection, *Filthy Labors,* a series of poems about her work at a transitional housing program for unwed mothers, is forthcoming from Northwestern University Press/Curbstone Press in 2017. Her website is www.laurenmarieschmidt.com.

BJ Ward is the author of four books of poetry, most recently *Jackleg Opera: Collected Poems 1990-2013.* His poems have appeared in *Poetry, American Poetry Review, TriQuarterly, The New York Times, The Normal School,* and *The Sun.* He is the recipient of a Pushcart Prize and two Distinguished Artist Fellowships from the NJ State Council on the Arts. His website is www.bj-ward.com.

Michael Waters' books include *Celestial Joyride* (2016), *Gospel Nights* (2011), *Darling Vulgarity* (2006—finalist for the *Los Angeles Times* Book Prize) and *Parthenopi: New and Selected Poems* (2001—finalist for the Paterson Poetry Prize) from BOA Editions. He has co-edited *Contemporary American Poetry* (Houghton Mifflin, 2006) and *Perfect in Their Art: Poems on Boxing from Homer to Ali* (Southern Illinois UP, 2003). Recipient of five Pushcart Prizes and fellowships from the NEA, Fulbright Foundation and NJ State Council on the Arts, Waters teaches at Monmouth University and in the Drew University MFA Program in Poetry & Poetry in Translation.

Daniel Weeks's latest collection of poems is *Self-Symphonies* (Blast Press, 2014). His poetry has been published in *The Cimarron Review, Mudfish, Puckerbrush Review, Zone 3, Slant, The Roanoke Review,* and many other literary journals. Two of his poems recently appeared in *Wild Poets of Ecstasy: An Anthology of Ecstatic Poetry* (Pelican Pond, 2011).

Joe Weil is an assistant professor at Binghamton University. His reviews, essays, poems and short stories have appeared in *Paterson Literary Review, The Literati Quarterly, Rattle, Barnstorm, Blue Collar Review, Lips, The Boston Review, North American Review, Omniverse,* the *New York Times, The Louisiana Review,* and *The Saranac Review,* among many others. He has four full-length collections of poetry; his latest collection of poems is *The Great Grandmother Light* published by New York Quarterly Books. In 2013 he was the recipient of the People's Poetry Award by Partisan Press. He has work forthcoming in *Chicago Quarterly Review,* a book of poetry, *Dialing the Light* forthcoming with New York Quarterly Books, and a book of instructive essays, *A Necessary Practice* forthcoming with BVT Publishing in January of 2016. Joe Weil co-founded Monk books with Bianca Stone and Adam Fitzgerald. He has since created Cat in the Sun books with his wife Emily Vogel. Having grown up in Elizabeth, New Jersey, Weil now lives in Binghamton with Emily and two small children, Clare and Gabriel.

Daniel Zimmerman teaches English at Middlesex County College, and co-edits *Middlesex: a literary journal.* The Institute of Further Studies included his fascicle, *Perspective,* in its series, *a curriculum of the soul* (Canton, NY: 1974). He collaborated with artist Richard Sturm on *See All the People* (Toronto: Open Studio/Scarborough College, 1976; available as an iBook). Pavement Saw Press published his *Post-Avant* as an Editor's Choice (Columbus, OH: 2002; introduction by Robert Creeley), and some of his anagrammatical poems, *ISOTOPES2,* appeared in 2007 (beardofbees.com). He edited NJCEA's *College English Notes,* and has published in several magazines and anthologies.

Jersey Shore Poets Acknowledgements

Christopher Bogart
"A Poem is a Stone": *Spindrift, A Book of Poetry* (2006)
"In the Gloaming": *Poetsonline.com* (July, 2008)
"Maypops": *The Whirlwind Review* (2014)
"Pony Ride": *The Monmouth Review* (Fall, 2013)
"Rose Garden": *Saggio Poetry Journal* (Fall, 2008)
"The Eater of Dreams": *This Broken Shore* (Summer, 2015)
"The Kill": *The Whirlwind Review* (2014)

Victoria Kaloss
"Sandy's Been Here": *Howl of Sorrow: A Collection of Poetry Inspired by Hurricane Sandy* (2015)
"Odyssey": *Wicked Banshee Press; Survivor Issue* (Fall, 2014)
"Extras Needed": *Poetic Reflections of Monmouth County* (2004)

Jerome Leary
"Seascape": *Monastic Muse New Skete,* (1996)
"River Library": *Published by Red Bank Library*
"Ocean Grove: a Psalm": *Spindrift, A Book of Poetry* (2006)
"Bloomfield Avenue": *Exit 13* (November, 2009)
"A Psalm": *Review for Religious* (July/August, 1991)
"Guest Room": *Voices Rising From The Grove* (2005)
"Before the Parkway": *Poetic Reflections of Monmouth County* (2004)
"First Snowfall": *Poetic Muse Winter* (1997)

Susan Martin
"A Dark Premonition": *Weirdyear* (January, 2012)
"When Frank Plays the Clarinet": *Still Crazy Literary Magazine: Volume VII, Issue 2,* (July, 2014)
"Whale Song": *Foliate Oak Literary Magazine* (April, 2013)

"Accounts Receivable": *Global Poets* (October, 2009)
"Gifts": *Epiphany Magazine: Issue 14* (October 21, 2012)
"Kvell": *Drash Anthology: Volume VI* (2012)
"No Atheists in Fox Holes": *Poetica Magazine* (Summer, 2010)
"Sing the Ballad": *Foliate Oak Literary Magazine* (April, 2013)
"Witches' Brew": *Society of Classical Poets* (Winter, 2017)

Linda Johnston Muhlhausen
"Reply to Jennifer": *Pedestal Magazine* (2007)
"Pectus Excavatum": *This Broken Shore* (2016)

Visiting Writers Acknowledgements

James Arthur
"Ode to an Encyclopedia": *Academy of American Poets' Poem-A-Day Project*

Renée Ashley
"Salt to Make a Sea": *The View from the Body*, Black Lawrence Press (2016)

Emanuel di Pasquale
"Loose Horse": *Poems in Sicily and America*, BLAST PRESS (2016)
"Meeting": *Poems in Sicily and America*, BLAST PRESS (2016)

Melissa Febos
"Chambermaid": *The Southeast Review*

Frank Finale
"Worm": *To The Shore Once More, Volume III*, Jersey Shore Publications (2016)

Penny Harder
"Darning Socks": *Verse-Virtual* (January 2016)

Lois Marie Harrod
"Like a Maelstrom with a Notch": *Naugatuck River Review*

John Hoppenthaler
"Dolphins at Point Pleasant Beach": *Lives Of Water*, Carnegie Mellon University Press (2003)

X. J. Kennedy
"Thomas Hardy's Obsequies": *Chautauqua* Magazine, and to be included in *That Swing: Poems 2008-2016,* Johns Hopkins University Press (2017)

Adele Kenny
"Without Seeing": *A Lightness, A Thirst, or Nothing At All,* Welcome Rain Publishers, New York, New York (2015)

Ted Kooser
"After Years": *Delights & Shadows* (2004)

Diane Lockward
"Invective Against the Bumblebee": *What Feeds Us,* Wind Publications (2006)

Donald "D. J." Moores
"The Problem of Rapture in the Literature Classroom": *This Broken Shore* (2016)

Mihaela Moscaliuc
"How to Ask for My Hand at My Grandmother's Grave": *Father Dirt,* Alice James Books (2010)

Peter E. Murphy
"Labor Day: Atlantic City": *Rattle, Poets Respond* (September 7, 2014)
http://www.rattle.com/labor-day-atlantic-city-by-peter-e-murphy/

Robert Pinsky
"At Pleasure Bay": *The Want Bone,* Farrar, Straus and Giroux (1991), first published in *The New Yorker*

Susanna Rich
"Hurry Up, Sunrise: Ocean Grove": *Urthona: A Journal of Cultural Renewal* (UK).

Christine Salvatore
"Leaving Town": *The Cortland Review, Issue 31*

B.J. Ward
"And All the Peasants Cheered for the King. The End": *Jackleg Opera: Collected Poems, 1990 to 2013,* North Atlantic Books (2013)

Michael Waters
"Cad": *The Hopkins Review* (Spring 2016)

Daniel Zimmerman
"winging it": *Indian Rope Trick,* Lakewood, OH: House Organ #9 (1994)

Whys & Wherefores

MEET ME IN BOTSWANA: WHAT IS BLAST PRESS?

A speech for national poetry month about BLAST PRESS.

Ab li dolen in l'air [look up: beauty falls from the air]
"A book should be a ball of light in your hands."
~~Ezra Pound

As we all know, April is "International Guitar Month."
But my heart twangs for poetry, and I was invited here to tell
you a little bit about a tiny poetry publishing company called
BLAST PRESS.
Description of BLAST PRESS
BLAST PRESS is what I would call a "micro-publisher."
We usually publish chapbooks—booklets under 100 pages in
length. Our print runs are usually under 100 copies per
edition. And BLAST PRESS has published over 100
chapbooks from some 20 authors in its career. The entire cost
is assumed by BLAST PRESS, so we are the publisher, and not
a vanity press or service.
BLAST PRESS has been sustaining its small operation—
in the black, mind you, no small feat—for about 20 years now.
We have had a few more ambitious titles where the book itself,
the author, and BLAST PRESS decide to dedicate the extra
resources needed to make the event a success.
Part of the BLAST PRESS ethos is to keep the authors in
charge of their work so that they can maintain maximum
control of their creative material in the out-lying years and
don't need to be writing to BLAST PRESS for permission to
re-publish snippets or poems.

BLAST PRESS

Our Credo
Do not dispraise the light
That, singing whatever's brightest,
Undoes the theft of night—
—Touch to caress, or move to love,
As this thoughtless rhyme does prove.

From Ascent

A SOLITARY HEADSTONE
Niggling addendum to "Meet me in Botswana"

Magazines, published with a week's, month's, quarter's or even a year's date grow elderly on the shelves in a way that a collection of one individual's work never can. What year does Shakespeare's book expire? Horace is renewed year by year, no matter how worn his saws may wane. But a magazine or casual collection of miscellaneous artifacts, no matter how august the individual members of the find, retain an interest for us mostly as a time capsule. Even the Egyptian tombs of the pharaohs hold more interest for us because of what they reveal about the era of their creation than for what they say about their putative occupants. Old poetry quarterlies are no different, although they may contain an Endymion.

This is why BLAST PRESS is dedicated to publishing single-author volumes and stand-alone essay collections almost exclusively. Unless a poet is unknown, there is no point in his publication being undertaken by a small press. And if an author is unknown, he is best presented to an unacquainted public in his own exclusive company. It is always wisest to let a guest unroll at least a few of his favorite tales before we escort him from the house. What is characteristic and worthwhile in the poet's voice will quietly assert itself over the course of his varied pieces much better than if we merely heard his alba or evensong in isolation, let alone in the cacophonous squawk of a miscellany. To the marriage of true minds, ours and the author's, let not serial publication admit impediments.

Only appearing in magazines and periodicals is like never having a final resting place—a poet without a plot.

Also Available

The Giant in the Cradle
Gregg Glory
[Gregg G. Brown]

List Price: $4.50
5.06" x 7.81"
Black & White on Cream
136 pages
ISBN-13: 978-1492396055
ISBN-10: 1492396052
BISAC: Poetry / American

FROM THE POEM "HEIGHT OF SUMMER"

Here is the day, the bridal day undaunted;
Here noon, at highest noon... hesitates...
The height of summer, at its crest arrested,
Held between warm hands to kiss—
The levitated real at pause in sun's perfection;
Paused because we cannot see, cannot imagine
Beyond such ripeness—

Yoga Notes
Carrie Pedersen Hudak

List Price: $4.50
5" x 8"
66 pages
ISBN-13: 978-1494330958
ISBN-10: 1494330954
BISAC: Body, Mind & Spirit

From the first essay: Just Practice

When I tell people I am a yoga teacher, they often say, I could never do yoga. I can't even touch my toes. Great, I say, you are already practicing awareness, that's part of the practice. Can you breathe? If you can breathe, then you can do yoga.

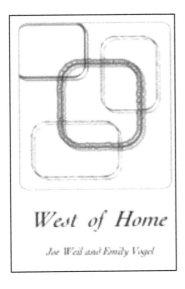

West of Home
Joe Weil, Emily Vogel

List Price: $10.00
Paperback: 98 pages
ISBN-10: 0615878415
ISBN-13:9780615878416
8 x 5 inches

From the Introduction

"West of Home" is a collaborative book of poetry which reflects the present and ongoing sentiments of Joe Weil and Emily Vogel. It includes 14 "responsorial" poems (call and response), between the two poets, as they respond to one another's themes and ideas, as well as two sections of poems, one for each poet's individual work.

Self-Symponies
Daniel Weeks

List Price: $10.00
Paperback: 146 pages
ISBN-10: 0692238581
ISBN-13: 978-0692238585
7.4 x 9.7 inches

From the Introduction

Inspired by listening to the four symphonies of Johannes
Brahms, Daniel Weeks's Self-Symphonies explore the
landscapes, cityscapes, and seascapes that are the
backdrop to a life lived on the New Jersey shore. The four
long poems in this collection provide meditations on
family, inheritance, and loss, society, nature, and culture,
and stasis and change—all of the elements that Coleridge
said bething the individual self.

The Pilot Light
Gregg Glory
[Gregg G. Brown]

List Price: $5.50
Paperback: 132 pages
ISBN-13: 9781511941921
5.5 x 8.5 inches

About *The Pilot Light*

The poems in Gregg Glory's The Pilot Light are about
relationships—with family, friends, and lovers—along
with reminiscences of a childhood spent close to nature in
the New Jersey countryside. Glory is particularly adept at
exploring the significant and oftentimes intimate moments
that define our most important relationships, moments
which, in turn, help us create the story of the self.

Knowing the Moment
Emanuel di Pasquale

List Price: $12.95
Paperback: 131 pages
ISBN-13: 9781503117471
5.5 x 8.5 inches

About *Knowing the Moment*

Emanuel di Pasquale has never been one to shy away from
the more difficult aspects of living a full and engaged
human life, and Knowing the Moment is perhaps his most
searing work in this regard, as he confronts the hardships
he encountered while growing up in his native Sicily. But
these kinds of revelations are never the final word in his
poetry. Tough times always seem to point him back to
love—as he casts his mind back to life in Sicily or engages
with the present in his poems about Long Branch, N.J.

**The Hummingbird's
Apprentice**
Gregg Glory
[Gregg G. Brown]

List Price: $4.50
Paperback: 159 pages
ISBN-10: 1511941928
ISBN-13: 9781511941921
5.1 x 7.8 inches

From *The Hummingbird's Apprentice*

ROADSIDE WINE

Pull off 71 suddenly, onto
a wide shoulder of dust and grass.
weigh down a length
of brown barbwire fence
like a wave of honey breaking.
Excited, splash ankle-deep
into the unhurrying surf
full of velvety bee sounds, and select
one perfect blossom. It is
so sweet in the slow afternoon.
And, where you've cut your thumb,
a thrill of air catches.

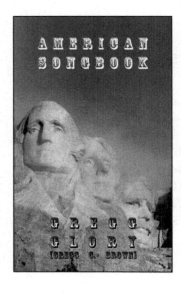

American Songbook
Gregg Glory
[Gregg G. Brown]

List Price: $3.75
Paperback: 98 pages
ISBN-10: 1482703297
ISBN-13: 9780692238585
5.5 x 8.5 inches

The Old Truculence

A note concerning the basic arc of this book of poems—to re-register grace and freedom as America's primary metier.

Freedom breeds elegance. Not the inbred elegance of aristocracy, where beautiful ladies eventually come to resemble their Russian wolfhounds. Nor, simply, the truculent elegance of that sly Benjamin Franklin who, as ambassador to the French Court, refused to bow before King Louis the 16th or doff his coonskin cap.

Freedom breeds the desire to create one meaningful action with your entire life—the effortful elegance of the artist that James Joyce defined as the willingness to gamble your whole life on the wrong idea, a bad aesthetic, or, it may be, a genuine triumph. And America has created, and can still create, a unique scale of opportunity for such elegant "throws of the dice," as Mallarme might say. A natty Fred Astaire (originally Austerlitz), gliding with the ease of an ice skater as he backs Rita Hayworth (a gal from Brooklyn) into immortality to a tune penned by the Jewish Jerome Kern in an industry patented in the U.S.A. is but one example of the scale of that opportunity.

When you are free to do anything, a desire grows in the breast not to do just anything, but to do the best thing—and that is an aesthetic dilemma. The mere accumulation of capital, or the arbitrary exercise by minor government regulators of petty power, are two classic examples of the desire for a meaningful expression of life-status that lack the aesthetic instinct. Such timid ambitions grow most strongly where the full range of light is narrowed, and the blossom of selfhood must twist around corners to open its ruby glory in a thinning patch of sunlight.

Gregg Glory
March, 2013

Come, My Dreams
Come gather round me, multitudinous dreams
That in the dim twilight are murmuring soft;
Come lay by my head in the pillow-seam;
Come carry my freighted heart aloft.

O, I would dare dream as few men dream
Beyond the cruel cudgel of the strong,
Beyond the purpled tapestries of is and seems
Hung before my eyes, beyond cold right or wrong.

Made in the USA
Columbia, SC
09 March 2018